IRISH COASTAL WALKS

A monument to countless Irish emigrants from Cobh

IRISH COASTAL WALKS

by
Paddy Dillon

CICERONE PRESS LTD
MILNTHORPE, CUMBRIA, UK

ISBN 1 85284 287 3
A catalogue copy of this book is available from the British Library.

Advice to Readers

Readers are advised that whilst every effort is taken by the author to ensure the accuracy of this guidebook, changes can occur which may affect the contents. It is advisable to check locally on transport, accommodation, shops etc but even rights-of-way can be altered.

The publisher would welcome notes of any such changes

Other Cicerone books by the same author:

The Irish Coast to Coast Walk

The Mountains of Ireland

Walking in the Isle of Arran

Walking in the Channel Islands

Walking in County Durham

Walking the GallowayHills

Walking in the North Pennines

Front cover: A walker stands close to the precipitous Cliffs of Moher

CONTENTS

INTRODUCTION 9
 Geology 9
 History 10
 Access 12
 Maps 12
 The Walks 13
 Getting to Ireland 13
 Getting around Ireland 14
 Accommodation 15
 Safety Matters 15

WALKS

 1 Donabate & Portrane 17
 2 Howth Head 20
 3 Bray Head 23
 4 Raven Point 26
 5 Carnsore Point 29
 6 Ardmore Head 34
 7 Great Island 37
 8 Sherkin Island 41
 9 Cape Clear Island 45
 10 Mizen Head 48
 11 Sheep's Head 50
 12 Bere Island 53
 13 Dursey Island 57
 14 Derrynane Bay 60
 15 Valentia Island 62
 16 Slea Head 65
 17 Great Blasket Island 69
 18 The Three Sisters 71
 19 The Magharees 74
 20 Kerry Head 77
 21 Loop Head 80

22   Cliffs of Moher 83
23   Inis Oírr 85
24   Inis Meáin 87
25   Inis Mór 90
26   Omey Island 95
27   Killary Harbour 97
28   Inishbofin 99
29   Inishturk 103
30   Clare Island 105
31   Minaun Cliffs 108
32   Croaghaun & Achill Head 111
33   Benwee Head 114
34   Belderrig to Portacloy 116
35   Downpatrick Head 121
36   Slieve League 123
37   Glencolmcille 127
38   Arranmore Island 130
39   Bloody Foreland 134
40   Tory Island 136
41   Horn Head 138
42   Melmore Head 141
43   Clonmany & Binnion 143
44   Malin Head 146
45   Inishowen Head 149
46   Castlerock & Downhill 151
47   Causeway Coast Path 153
48   Rathlin Island 159
49   Fair Head 163
50   Whitehead & Black Head 166
51   North Down Coast Path 168
52   Strangford Lough 172
53   Killough & Ballyhornan 176
54   Dundrum & Murlough 179

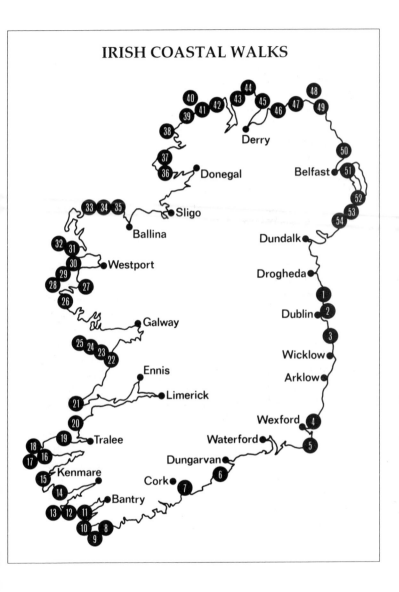

IRISH COASTAL WALKS

Heavy seas batter the cliffs on Valentia Island

INTRODUCTION

Ireland is a small country, but its coastline measures around 3,500 miles (5,600km). The western seaboard is incredibly convoluted, breaking into fine headlands and a spread of islands. While many parts of Ireland's coastline are well known, such as the Giant's Causeway and the Cliffs of Moher, few have heard of the Wexford Coastal Path, the Sheep's Head or Inishturk. This guide covers over fifty coastal walks around Ireland, taking in broad beaches, towering cliffs, battered headlands and a score of lovely islands. There is a huge amount of variety, astounding scenery, plenty of history and heritage, with a good system of transport, accommodation and other services. In sunshine or storm, many of these coastal walks exhibit a raw, rare beauty.

GEOLOGY
The geology of a coastline stretching for thousands of miles is not a subject which can be adequately discussed in a few words. However, there are some sweeping generalisations which can be made. Ireland is saucer-shaped, with a broad, rolling central plain. All around this, and so all around the coast, are ranges of hills and fine mountains. As a result, the coastline often features cliffs, hills and mountains. Generally, the western coast is more rugged than the eastern coast. The cliffs are often composed of igneous or metamorphic rocks, with some ancient sedimentary strata. It is often the case that sedimentary strata feature parallel banded layers, which may be tilted or even tightly folded. Igneous and metamorphic rocks generally present a more fluid, amorphous structure.

A more recent occurrence has shaped the Irish coastline, and that is the Ice Age. Ice covered much of Ireland and glaciers scoured great troughs from the mountains and smoothed much of the rock around the coast. It also dumped masses of crushed rock and boulders which has since been shaped by the action of the sea into bouldery, cobbly and sandy beaches. The end of the Ice Age brought a rise in the sea level, which separated Ireland from Britain and the rest of Europe. The lifting of the weight of ice from the land also resulted in the shifting of Ireland's bedrock, which actually 'floats'

The geology of the Giant's Causway is quite amazing

in the deeper and slightly plastic mantle of the Earth. This shifting is called 'isostatic recovery' and has resulted in Ireland having a definite north-south tilt. The practical upshot is that the northern coasts feature raised beaches and the southern coasts feature drowned river valleys. Strangely enough, this influences access in an important way. Southern landscapes can be farmed practically down to the sea, while northern landscapes generally end with a cliff-line, or a rugged raised beach unsuitable for cultivation.

HISTORY
In the ancient epic legends of most countries there is a creation myth, but not so in Ireland. In the beginning Ireland was already there; already an island awaiting its first inhabitants. Naturally they came off the sea; wave after wave of invaders, slaughtering and conquering each other. *Leabha Gabhala Eirinn* or the *Book of the Takings of Ireland* is full of stirring stuff and contains many coastal

references. Ireland was an island before it was colonised by people. Two things are for certain: anyone colonising Ireland came from the sea, and their first experience of the country was of its coast. Other things are less certain: Did Amergin the Poet really chant Ireland into existence from the sea? Was the sea really black with the ships of the King of the World before the Battle of Ventry Strand? Did Brendan the Navigator, a native of Kerry, really discover America before Columbus?

> 'Ireland is a melting pot of conquered cultures, stone men and bronze men and iron men, of Celts and Vikings and Anglo-Normans, driven remorselessly westwards by a volcano of European history, pressed finally together against the rim of the Atlantic in their promontory forts, between the devil of the new weapon and the deep sea. Their Gods go with them. Duk Duk dancers and Druids, Fir Bolg and Tuatha De Danann, Baal and Beltaine, Crom Cruach and Cromwell, the conquered conquerors, enslaved, revengeful charged with ancient powers.'
>
> T.H. White, *The Godstone and the Blackymor*.

Centuries of British dominance in Ireland have shaped the development of the coastline and the Irishman's relationship with the sea. There is no doubt that the people of Ireland have always been among the world's most skilful seamen, coursing their canvas curraghs over the most tempestuous seas. While neighbouring Britain developed as a major seafaring power, Ireland was held in check. Ireland's great seafarers and fishermen were not allowed to create a naval force or great fishing fleets. Port developments were few, and of limited extent.

Stout, stone Martello Towers and the square towers of old signal stations were built in the 19th century, with early radio stations being sited along the west coast of Ireland in the early 20th century. Only in recent decades have decent little piers and slipways become common. With the wane of British influence in Ireland, ending only with the handing over of the 'Treaty Ports' in 1938, the development of Ireland as a maritime power has been limited. What remains, therefore, is a coastline largely free of large-scale developments, abounding in natural beauty.

11

ACCESS

It may seem strange in a country where interest in walking is developing apace to discover that there is no clear policy on access, and very little legislation. In Northern Ireland, the Access to the Countryside (1983) Order provides the framework for developing and regulating access, with most of the responsibilities devolved onto the District Councils. In the Republic of Ireland, there is no overall legislation governing access, so that the public have to rely on common law principles, and in case of difficulty, the vagaries of the court system. The 1995 Occupier's Liability Act, which was supposed to protect landowners against claims for injury from the public, has actually led to the withdrawal of access in many areas. While many parts of the coast are eminently accessible, there are other areas where there is very little access. There are a few popular places where traditional access routes to or along the coast are being challenged.

Generally speaking, if there is any real objection to you following the coast anywhere around Ireland, it should be patently obvious. Any discussion of access issues quickly becomes mired in a swamp of legal complexities involving insurance, liability and property ownership rights; issues which most walkers from most parts of the world would find baffling. Ireland has no cogent legislation dealing with access to the countryside, and it is unlikely that visiting walkers will be able to make any sense of the situation.

MAPS

The maps in this guide are basic sketch maps which show the difference between the land and the sea, and show which parts of the routes are on paths, roads or along the shore. These maps need to be used alongside the appropriate Ordnance Survey maps. Maps in the Republic of Ireland are published by the Ordnance Survey of Ireland, while in Northern Ireland they are published by the Ordnance Survey of Northern Ireland. The entire coastline is covered by 1:50,000 scale maps. The Discovery Series in the Republic of Ireland and Discoverer Series in Northern Ireland are numbered according to an all-Ireland index. The Aran Islands off the western coast are covered by a 1:25,000 scale OS map. The appropriate sheet numbers for all maps needed are given in the introductions to each of the routes. There are 39 maps covering the coast out of the full quota of 89 maps in the 1;50,000 Discovery/Discoverer Series.

THE WALKS

The walks are of course all coastal. However, they are also remarkably varied and represent a good selection of routes which include cliffs and rocky headlands, marshes, dunes and estuaries, with plenty of wilderness and little industry. The classic coastal names are there: Bray Head, the Cliffs of Moher, the Giant's Causeway, etc. A spread of fascinating islands include: the Aran Islands, Clare Island, Achill Island, Tory Island and Rathlin. In fact, there are a total of 54 coastal walks including 19 walks on islands. Most of the walks are quite easy, but some are more akin to mountain walks, climbing over some of the highest sea cliffs in Europe. The walks are numbered and arranged in a clockwise direction around the coast, starting north of Dublin, taking in the eastern, southern and western coasts, ending in Northern Ireland. There is a distinct bias towards the western seaboard.

GETTING TO IRELAND

There have never been so many fast and frequent options for reaching Ireland as at present. Basically, you need to decide if you are taking your car across on a ferry, hiring a car on arrival, or using public transport. Car ferries operate between Britain and Ireland from Holyhead to Dublin and Dun Laoghaire; Pembroke and Fishguard to Rosslare; Swansea to Cork; Stranraer to Larne and Belfast; Liverpool to Belfast; and even a summer service from Campbeltown to Ballycastle. The only real ferry links with mainland Europe and Ireland are the summer services between Le Havre and Rosslare, St. Malo and Cork.

Flights operate from many British airports to most Irish airports, giving entry options as varied as Dublin, Waterford, Cork, Kerry, Shannon, Galway, Knock, Donegal and Derry. If arriving by air, check in advance if the smaller airports have onward bus or taxi services. Flights from further afield in Europe or from the rest of the world are likely to touch down only at airports such as Dublin, Belfast or Shannon.

It's possible to book through tickets on rail, bus and ferries between Britain and Ireland. Rail enquiry offices and major bus stations can often supply details and sometimes there are astoundingly cheap return fares. Few people realise, for instance, that there are daily bus services from London to points along the west coast of Ireland. Nor are people generally aware of how easily they can access the most remote walks in the west of Ireland by flying direct from many British airports.

GETTING AROUND IRELAND

Cars can be used to reach most of the coastal walks, but it won't be possible to take them across to some of the islands. Car parks are noted at the start of the walks where appropriate; sometimes they can be quite large at popular destinations, but at other places they may be quite small. You take your chances at busy times, especially in the summer months, when some of them become quite full.

Bus services could be used to reach the majority of the walks, and with careful reference to timetables you can get away again afterwards. More rarely, trains can be used to get to and from coastal walks, but this is really only an option near the cities of Dublin, Cork and Belfast. As the range of public transport options is really quite large, yet little appreciated, details are given in the introductions to the walks. Bus Eireann covers virtually the whole of the Republic of Ireland, though Lough Swilly Buses are more common around Donegal. Ulsterbus covers the whole of Northern Ireland. Trains are operated by Iarnrod Eireann in the Republic of Ireland and Northern Ireland Railways in the north. Both bus and rail services sometimes operate across the border. Bus and rail tickets are available in a number of forms, offering anything from a week to a month of travelling on one or both sides of the border on buses, trains or both. The vast majority of walks in this book were covered using bus and rail services.

Contact: Bus Eireann, Dublin, 01 8366111.
            Swilly Bus, Derry, 028 7126 2017.
            Ulsterbus, Belfast, 028 9033 3000.
            Iarnrod Eireann, Dublin, 01 8366222.
            Northern Ireland Railways, Belfast, 028 9089 9411.

ACCOMMODATION

Generally, there is no shortage of accommodation around the Irish coast. In fact, you'll often be spoilt for choice, with options including campsites, hostels, B&Bs, guesthouses, inns and hotels. However, bear in mind that there are some very wild stretches of coastline where you could walk most of the day without passing any accommodation. Although there is a very wide choice, bear in mind the seasonal nature of the business. Everywhere will be open in the height of summer, but as a consequence most places will be full. In the winter months many places may be closed. The shoulder seasons offer the best chance to drift into most types of acccommodation, and the weather is often very pleasant for walking.

Accommodation options can be checked or booked in advance by referring to a variety of lists, brochures and booklets. If the process becomes too bewildering, then the tourist information offices will be pleased to assist. Bord Failte (Irish Tourist Board) and the Northern Ireland Tourist Board can offer help and advice, or make bookings on your behalf, and they work very closely together these days. They will always book you into places which are 'approved' and conform to certain standards.

SAFETY MATTERS

While most of these walks are quite easy and straightforward, some of them feature unguarded cliffs and rugged, pathless slopes. The route descriptions give an indication of the nature of the terrain, but there are other factors to take into account. Time and tide, they say, wait for no-one, and the weather is similarly beyond your control. At the outset, if the walk is partly along the beach or shore, then check the local tide tables. You may have to postpone your walk, or choose another route, but it's better than being forced inland across awkward fences and ditches, or worse, to be drowned! On steep slopes and cliffs, rain can make the ground muddy and slippery, while strong winds can occasionally bowl a walker over, which could have fatal consequences. On some of the islands, adverse weather can bring a halt to all ferry services, and in extreme instances you could be marooned for a week or more! For this reason, most of the islands which are visited offer food, drink and accommodation.

If the worst comes to the worst and either you or someone else needs urgent assistance, the whole of the Irish coast has a good level of rescue cover. Some parts are accessible to vehicles, but there are sea and cliff rescue teams, with helicopters on standby. All emergency services, including the police (Garda or RUC), ambulance, coastguard, sea and cliff rescue, are alerted by dialling 999 from any telephone. Be ready to give full details of the emergency and follow any instructions you are given.

Ruined signal towers are dotted around the Irish coast

THE WALKS

WALK 1
Donabate and Portrane

It's not immediately apparent just how much coastal walking can be enjoyed from Donabate, but there is access to a fine cliff walk with a view towards Lambay Island, and there are two broad estuaries penetrating far inland. The coast exhibits a variety of landforms including mudflats, sand dunes, cliffs and caves. There are also interesting heritage details which include two Martello towers and a round tower. The sheltered mudflats of the Rogerstown Estuary form a notable bird reserve.

The Route

Distance:	8 miles (13 kilometres).
Start:	Donabate Station - 227499.
Maps:	OS Discovery Sheets 43 & 50.
Terrain:	Easy shoreline roads and a well trodden cliff path.
Parking:	Beside Donabate Station.
Transport:	Dublin Bus 33B and Suburban Rail services.

Start at the railway station in Donabate. Follow the main road away from the village, but note St. Patrick's Church of Ireland off to the right, with its attractive semi-ruined tower. Turn left at a road junction signposted for the Island Golf Club. This road runs under a railway bridge, then continues beside the saltings of the Malahide Estuary. The piping of curlews and the peeping of sandpipers are common sounds across the water or mudflats.

Pass Meadow Lodge, where the farm is dominated by a curious concrete tower. Further along the road, to the left, is a cutting in a roughly bedded glacial till. At the next road junction, keep straight on as signposted for the Corballis Public Golf Course. The road passes Balcarrick Golf Course too. Note the Mandarin Restaurant with its carved granite Chinese lions on guard. Turn right at the next road junction to reach The Dunes Hotel, beach car park, toilets and a stout Martello Tower. A notice beside the car park points out that

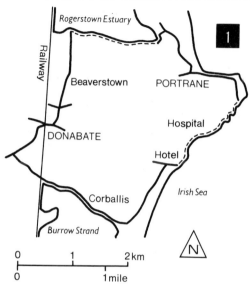

sandwich terns and brent geese can be observed along Donabate Beach. There are views of Lambay Island, Howth Head and Ireland's Eye.

Walk in front of the hotel, picking up a grassy, sandy path above the low rock and shingle shore. Pass a couple of houses, then note the architecturally splendid redbrick hospital on the headland. (While looking very grand and ornate from the outside, parts of the inside are badly in need of repair). A large sign warns that part of the path ahead is dangerous, though this would seem a curious warning when comparing the path to some of the more rugged headland walks in this book. Follow a broad, grassy path for a short while, then continue along a narrower path with slabs sloping steeply seawards. There is a stout wall to follow, then one cliff-top stretch is fenced. The path soon reaches a car park and toilets, where a Martello Tower has been converted into a fine dwelling.

Follow the road past Lynders Caravan and Camping Park, reaching a green area near the beach at Portrane. The road runs straight to Grogan's store, where a right turn offers access to a ruined church with a leaning tower. Follow the road signposted The

The rugged cliffs at Portrane boast an excellent path

Burrows and note a ruined, ivy-clad castle off to the left. There is later a road turning off to the right, but keep straight on, then turn left where a narrow road is signposted as a cul-de-sac. The road leads down to the Rogerstown Estuary.

Follow the road to its end, then walk along the squelchy saltings. At very high tides this stretch might prove impassable. The estuary waters and mudflats extend to the right, while to the left grass gives way to thorny scrub, bushes and trees. Walk alongside the estuary until a road-end is reached, well before the Rogerstown Viaduct and a prominent tip head. Strange how tips and bird reserves are often found close together!

Follow the road inland, crossing a broad rise and passing the Beaverstown Golf Course and Tir Na Nog B&B. The road runs straight onwards, entering Donabate and passing Keelings Bar and a few shops. Turn right after the Catholic Church to reach Smyths Bar and the Post Office. A right turn leads straight down to Donabate Railway Station.

Lambay Island
There is evidence of human habitation on Lambay Island from Neolithic times, some 6,000 years ago. Although the island looks

19

well cultivated from afar, it is also a notable wildlife reserve. The cliffs are teeming with a variety of birds, as well as seals, while inland there are deer and even wallabies. Very few visitors are allowed ashore, though occasionally scientific or naturalist groups will be permitted to explore the island. The owner is Lord Revelstoke.

Rogerstown Estuary

Mudflats and saltings are a feature of the broad Rogerstown Estuary. There is a tip beyond the railway at the head of the estuary, which offers rich pickings for a variety of birds. The estuary is a site of international importance for brent geese.

WALK 2
Howth Head

Howth Head is a well-known landmark, passed by ferries and flights in and out of Dublin. Ptolemy recorded it as the island of Edros in the 4th century, although it is now joined to the mainland. Classic cliff walking can be enjoyed within sight of Dublin city. The circuit can be accomplished using a well-trodden path from Howth Harbour to the Baily Lighthouse, then another path continues round to Sutton. Although the suburbs of Dublin spread out to Sutton and Howth, the walk is surprisingly wild at times. Buses and trains offer easy access from the city and there is a chance to shorten the walk by heading inland from the Baily Lighthouse to link with a Dublin Bus service at The Summit.

The Route

Distance:	8 miles (13 kilometres).
Start:	Howth Harbour - 288393.
Map:	OS Discovery Sheet 50.
Terrain:	Well-trodden cliff paths, rugged in places, with roads towards the end.
Parking:	Large car park at Howth Harbour.
Transport:	Dublin Bus 31 & 31B and DART rail services.

If reaching Howth on the DART railway, turn left to leave the station to walk along Harbour Road. Dublin Bus services cover this

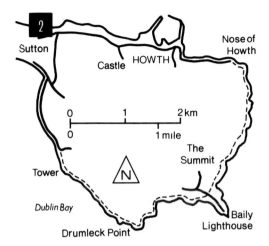

road, ending close to a large car park used by anyone arriving by car. Follow Harbour Road to the East Pier, then turn right and follow Balscadden Road uphill. Look back to the rocky little island of Ireland's Eye and beyond to the Mountains of Mourne. A Martello Tower stands at a higher level overlooking Balscadden Bay and Howth Harbour.

Follow the road marked as a cul de sac, passing Balscadden House, which was once the home of William Butler Yeats. Follow the road to its end, where there is a small parking space and a few buildings. Keep to the right of the buildings to follow a clear path beyond some bollards. The path climbs gently as it turns around the Nose of Howth. Although the path is well surfaced, there are rugged slopes above and below. After turning round the nose, there are views of the Wicklow Mountains across Dublin Bay. Killiney, Bray Head and Wicklow Head are arranged one after the other along the coast. Closer to hand, the cliff ledges may be teeming with kittiwakes and fulmars, with various divers below.

The Baily Lighthouse stands at the end of a rocky point and the cliff path starts to descend towards it, twisting and turning as it drops. Take care not to follow any other paths leading inland. Cross over the access road which serves the lighthouse and another well-trodden path will be found leading through dense bushes which look like garden escapees. Further along there is a view around the rugged Doldrum Bay, with the Baily Lighthouse to the left and a white cliff-top cottage to the right. The path runs behind the cottage and reaches a junction with another path. Turn right and note a metal plaque set into the ground reading: 'Right of way - Please do not throw stones over cliffs.'

The path is broad and clear, and gates to right and left lead into private gardens. Turn left at a junction of paths beside a short stretch of lapboard fencing and follow the path gently downhill. The path runs away from the garden hedges and crosses more open slopes. After turning round Drumleck Point there are no more views of the Baily Lighthouse, but the whole of Dublin Bay is stretched out in a vast panoramic sweep. Short flights of steps are used and the path follows a stout wall whose stones have been bonded with a rough seashell mortar. The path moves away from the wall while crossing a steep and rocky slope.

Look carefully ahead to keep the path in view, and if children are present then keep them close to hand. At one point you may need to use your hands for balance as your feet pick a way across a steep and rocky slope. An easier path continues towards a Martello Tower, and beyond the tower a clear track leads to a road.

Turn left to follow Strand Road, which has a Dublin Bus service, as well as a shop selling food and drink. Strand Road joins Carrickbrack Road, where a right turn is made. Later, turn left along the road called Offington Park; a pleasant, leafy, suburban road. A right turn at the end leads onto the busy Howth Road, which has a Dublin Bus service and the DART railway alongside. The DART station is passed before the harbour is reached; where shops, pubs and restaurants can be patronised. Short walks can be enjoyed along the West and East Piers, and there are sometimes ferry trips out to the rugged Ireland's Eye, which abounds in interest.

Balscadden House

The poet and playwright William Butler Yeats lived at Balscadden House from 1880 to 1883. A plaque records a few of his words, appropriate for anyone walking by: 'I have spread my dreams under your feet,' he wrote. 'Tread softly because you tread on my dreams.'

Howth Castle

Howth Castle is passed towards the end of the walk. It has been the seat of the St. Lawrence family for centuries. The sea-queen Granuaile (see Clare Island - Walk 30) came calling in 1575, but was left at the gate while the family dined. In a fury, she kidnapped the heir to the estate and shipped him round to Connacht. He was released unharmed when she had secured a promise that any O'Malley who called at mealtimes would be granted admission! The castle is also home to an interesting Transport Museum. Of particular note is a tram which once climbed to The Summit above the coastal path. There are also double-decker buses, fire engines, trucks and tractors; all nicely restored to tip-top vintage condition.

Ireland's Eye

Short ferry services from Howth Harbour can bring this rugged little island underfoot. The cliffs are home to a variety of birds, while the interior is ungrazed and quite overgrown. St. Nessan's Church is all that remains of an early Christian community which was established in the 6th century. There is also a Martello Tower on the island.

WALK 3

Bray Head

The southward growth of Bray as a Victorian seaside resort was arrested by the rugged cliffs of Bray Head. However, a railway was cut along the base of the cliffs, leading to the next coastal village of Greystones. The railway is accompanied by a fine path, though there are other paths which climb over the rugged summit of Bray Head. The walk from Bray to Greystones or vice versa is a popular choice among locals, and visitors will find it easy and interesting. The walk is described from station to station.

The Route

Distance:	6 miles (10 kilometres).
Start:	Bray Railway Station - 270187.
Finish:	Greystones Railway Station - 297122.

Map:	OS Discovery Sheet 56.
Terrain:	Very clear and well-trodden cliff paths.
Parking:	In Bray town centre or at the end of Putland Road, and around Greystones.
Transport:	DART services to Bray and Suburban Rail back from Greystones. Dublin Bus 45, 45A, 84 & 85 to Bray.

Leave the DART railway station and cross a nearby level crossing, then follow the promenade running parallel to the Esplanade

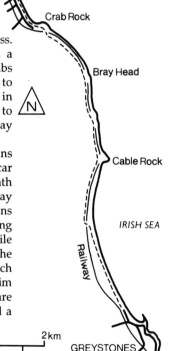

towards Bray Head. The rugged headland is unmistakable, being surmounted by a prominent cross. After passing the Bray Head Inn, a broad, curved concrete track climbs uphill and crosses a railway bridge to pass a car park. Motorists can park in town, or drive along Putland Road to reach the car park at the foot of Bray Head.

The broad and clear cliff path runs parallel to the railway beyond the car park. (Off to the right is a stepped path climbing to the cross on top of Bray Head.) The cliff path is fenced and runs parallel to the railway, often running almost vertically above the lines. While marvelling at the engineering of the railway, note also an abandoned stretch of cuttings and a tunnel, which fell victim to coastal erosion. The rock walls are like hanging gardens in places, and a few sure-footed wild goats might be spotted. Guano-stained rocks are the preserve of a variety of gulls, while some tidal rocks may be used as perches by cormorants drying their wings. Views northwards along the coast reveal Dalkey Island, Howth Head and Lambay Island.

The cliff path passes some farmland, rising to the right, and the way is enclosed with trees and shrubs for a short while. The path drops from rocky slopes onto glacial till, which shows several signs of collapse. For proof of continuing erosion, there is one stretch where there are four parallel lines of retreating wire fencing! Despite the crumbling cliffs, walkers keep treading a path and this is enclosed by stout fencing. There are views inland of the rugged hills of Little and Great Sugar Loaf.

Sports pitches are passed, followed by angling and yacht club premises. Keep left along the coastal road in Greystones, passing restaurants, a take-away and La Touche Hotel. The road swings inland near Greystones Railway Station, and by crossing a footbridge or nearby level crossing a full range of shops, pubs and restaurants can be discovered in the centre of town, as well as the main entrance to the railway station.

Bray Heritage Centre
Housed in the fine old Courthouse on Main Street, dating from 1841, the Bray Heritage Centre details the growth of the former market town and its transformation into one of Ireland's premier seaside resorts. In the late 19th century whole terraces of hotels and guesthouses were constructed, and the place still has an air of Victoriana. The tourist information office is also located in the building.

The National Aquarium
Featuring native and imported fish, the National Aquarium on the Esplanade is rather larger than you might anticipate. There are over 200 tanks holding some 10,000 fish, made up of more than 700 species. While many of the exotic imported species attract most attention, take the time to study the native Irish species, and particularly those from the sea, as they won't be seen quite so easily on any of the coastal walks!

Greystones

Greystones takes its name from the Grey Stones above the little harbour. The railway helped it to become a seaside resort, and as it is now well connected with Dublin, it is developing into something of a commuter suburb.

WALK 4
Raven Point

Curracloe Beach is a popular summertime choice for holidaymakers in the south-east of Ireland. The Raven Nature Reserve stretches southwards as a forested area of sand dunes sheltering the reclaimed Wexford Sloblands. The Wexford Coastal Path makes a complete circuit around The Raven, continuing inland through the village of Curracloe. Nearby attractions include the Wexford Wildfowl Reserve and the historic town of Wexford, both of which are in view from the route.

The Route

Distance:	6 miles (10 kilometres).
Start:	Curracloe Beach - 113266.
Map:	OS Discovery Sheet 77.
Terrain:	Dune path, sandy beach and forest track. Easy and level throughout.
Parking:	Beside the dunes and forest near Curracloe Beach.
Transport:	Bus Eireann table number 379 operates through Curracloe on Mondays and Saturdays only.

The Wexford Coastal Path is waymarked along the R741 and R743 roads from Wexford Bridge to Curracloe. Follow the 'man on water' signs from Curracloe to find a minor road leading to a car park near Curracloe Beach, at the entrance to the Raven Nature Reserve. There are a couple of corrugated tin chalets nearby.

A path made of wooden railway sleepers crosses the sand dunes to reach Curracloe Beach. Turn right through a gap in a wooden fence to follow a sandy dune path alongside a forest. The dunes rise

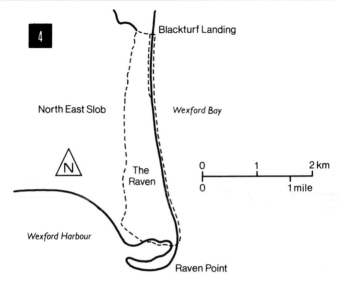

Blackturf Landing

North East Slob

Wexford Bay

The Raven

0   1   2 km

0   1 mile

Wexford Harbour

Raven Point

to either side of the path and are bound by moss and marram grass, with a good range of flora. The dunes tend to obscure a view of the sea, so either drift down to the shore, or follow the path onwards until forced onto the beach. The southern part of the dune belt has been eroded and some of the trees have toppled onto the beach, so walking along the sandy shore is the only way forward.

There are plenty of shells to study, and if the tide is at least part way out, then the sand is quite firm underfoot. Watch for a way back onto the dunes at the southern end of the forest. Just to sea, if the tide allows, you may spot the remaining spars of a wrecked ship. The path through the dunes hugs the edge of the forest, and there are views of the distant Tuskar Rock and its lighthouse; Greenore Point and Rosslare Harbour; Rosslare and Wexford Town.

A grassy, sandy track is drawn off the dunes and into the forest. Keep left to follow a gravel track further inland, taking advantage of wooden benches along the way if a rest is needed. Tall pines to the right have bird boxes nailed to them, while the ground is covered in bracken, brambles and ivy. The trees to the left are younger and more densely planted, but later there are some good views across

Galloping the horses along the sands at Raven Point

the level, reclaimed farmlands known as 'slobs'. The track leads out of the forest and back to the car park where the walk started.

Curracloe
The little village of Curracloe has a small range of useful services, including a pub, restaurant, take-away, shop and accommodation. Travelling through the countryside, there are a number of attractively thatched cottages. Walkers using the Bus Eireann service through Curracloe will need to follow roads out of the village and back later, at a cost of $2^{1}/_2$ miles (4 kilometres) extra.

Raven Nature Reserve
The varied habitats of the Raven Nature Reserve include a forestry plantation, dune belt, sandy beach and seabed. The dunes have a well-established flora including rarities such as wild asparagus, round-leaved wintergreen, lesser centuary and yellow birdnest.

The beach is littered with a fine assortment of shells. The detached southern dunes are frequented by Greenland white-fronted geese and waders, while terns are regular breeders. The Raven is twinned with Baie de la Canche in France and Dunas de San Jacinto in Portugal, as well as being a National Hare Reserve.

Wexford Wildfowl Reserve
Signposted from the Wexford to Curracloe road, the Wexford Wildfowl Reserve is situated on the reclaimed 'sloblands' north of Wexford Harbour. There are bird hides, an observation tower and a small visitor centre. The reserve is noted for its visiting Greenland white-fronted geese, as well as Canada, greylag and pink-footed geese. Ducks and waders are also common.

WALK 5
Carnsore Point

For a waymarked coastal path around a significant turning point on the Irish coast, with abundant connections from parts of Ireland, Britain and France, this can be a rather quiet walk. The Wexford Coastal Path enjoys its most significant off-road stretch between Rosslare Harbour and Kilmore Quay. Some parts are on good paths and tracks, but other parts are along sand, shingle or bouldery beaches. There are a couple of points where high tides could cause delays, but otherwise the route is mostly level and easy.

The Route

Distance:	18¹/₂ miles (30 kilometres).
Start:	Rosslare Harbour - 137125.
Finish:	Kilmore Quay - 965033.
Map:	OS Discovery Sheet 77.
Terrain:	Coastal paths, dune paths and beach walks. Can be quite bouldery in places.
Parking:	At Rosslare Harbour, and at most beach access points along the route.
Transport:	Direct ferry services from Fishguard, Pembroke and Le Havre. Rail services link with Dublin. Bus Eireann table

numbers 2, 40 & 55 serve Rosslare, while Kilmore Quay is
served by the more limited table number 383.

Start at the large ferry terminal building at Rosslare Harbour.
Follow the road inland only a short way from the car park. There is
a roundabout on the road, with an old railway turntable alongside.
A flight of steps are signposted for the Rosslare Harbour Youth
Hostel, which is close to the prominent Hotel Rosslare. Views
stretch from the Wicklow and Blackstairs Mountains to the Tuskar
Rock Lighthouse. There is a clear path to the left along the top of a
steep bank, then a flight of wooden steps leads down to the beach.

Turn right at the bottom of the steps and follow a sandy path
through marram grass to reach the shore. Continue along sand and
shingle beaches, passing the base of some slumping clay cliffs.
There is a significant turn round Greenore Point, which could be
impassable at high water. Cormorants are accustomed to perch on
tidal rocks and the prominent Carrick Beacon is offshore. After
walking round St. Helen's Bay, come ashore using a flight of steps
through thorny scrub, passing St. Helen's Cottages to continue
along a sandy track. There is a car park beside a bridge near a
concrete pier, then a sandy path leads up to St. Helen's Church.

Beyond St. Helen's, the narrow, sandy path can feel a bit heavy
underfoot, and beyond Old Mill it becomes rather overgrown, so it
is better to walk along the beach. There is plenty of firm sand
between the tidal limits passing Ballytrent on the way to Carne.
Come ashore before Carne to follow sandy paths and tracks from a
wooded area, passing a large caravan site, to reach a small harbour,

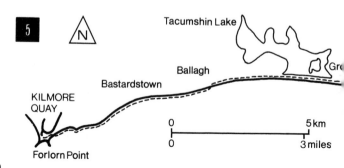

30

seen at the little harbour at Carne. It records that between the years 1859 and 1897 they made 34 launches and saved 130 lives.

Carnsore Point
There is a feeling of remoteness on this battered corner of Ireland. Several habitations were demolished when a nuclear power station was planned in the 1970s, but thankfully that was never built. One of the casualties might have been the ancient church and holy well dedicated to St. Vogue, all that remains of an early monastic site. A single headstone alongside the church is barely legible, but the words 'wrecked near Carnsore Point' can be deciphered. St. Vogue, or Veoc, may have been from south-west Britain and he died in Brittany in the year 585. Offshore, Tuskar Rock Lighthouse dates from 1815.

Lady's Island Lake
Lady's Island was the site of a monastery dedicated to the Blessed Virgin, on what was formerly a sea inlet. The lake is an important wildfowl reserve, and is the only place where gadwall regularly breed in Ireland. The islands of Inish and Sgharbheen are noted for their populations of breeding terns. This is the only place known in Ireland where all five Irish species are found breeding together. They include common, sandwich, arctic, little and roseate terns. A large gullery includes common and herring gulls, as well as greater and lesser black-backed gulls.

Kilmore Quay
This delightful village of thatched, whitewashed cottages (looking like ice-creams covered in thick chocolate sauce) is noted for its small fishing industry. There is an interesting maritime museum housed aboard the lightship 'Guillemot', which is now embedded in concrete on the harbourside. It was the last Irish lightship, and still has its original cabin, generators and fittings.

Saltee Islands
Saltee Island Big and Saltee Island Little lie close to Kilmore Quay. In the summer there are several trips either around the islands or landing for a short while. The islands form one of Ireland's largest bird sanctuaries, and seals are also commonly seen on their shores.

WALK 6
Ardmore Head

The short cliff walk around Ardmore Head and Ram Head could be completed in an hour from the little seaside resort of Ardmore, but there is a lot to see and you might need longer. Ardmore is the oldest Christian settlement in Ireland, dating from the early 5th century. A series of ancient structures can be inspected, and the well-maintained cliff path has been waymarked as part of St. Declan's Way, running inland to the celebrated Rock of Cashel.

The Route

Distance:	3 miles (5 kilometres).
Start:	Tourist information office at Ardmore - 192777.
Map:	OS Discovery Sheet 82.
Terrain:	A short and well-marked cliff path.
Parking:	Beside the tourist information office.
Transport:	Bus Eireann table numbers 260 & 362 serve Ardmore.

Start in Ardmore at the tourist information office. This curious building is shaped like a white sandcastle, standing beside the sea with car parking alongside. Follow the coastal road through town, which is signposted for St. Declan's Well and Cliff Walk. Pass St. Declan's Catholic Church, then note the steps going down to St. Declan's Stone on the shore. Follow the road above the harbour, passing a pottery and the Cliff Hotel. The road ends and the cliff path leads straight to St. Declan's Hermitage and Holy Well. There is an abundance of wild garlic along this stretch.

The path continues round Ardmore Head to a concrete lookout post. Nearby is a small crenelated building known as The Castle, while further beyond is the old Coastguard Station; both dating from 1867. Views from Ardmore Head stretch from Mine Head in the east to Capel Island off Youghal and the more distant Ballycotton Island to the west. Down below, where it was wrecked in a rocky cove in 1987, is the rusting crane ship 'Samson', surrounded by screaming gulls.

Continue round the rocky Ram's Head, passing the curious

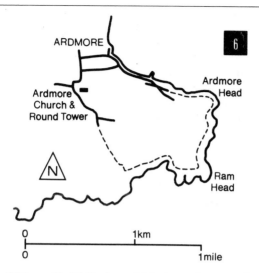

Father O'Donnell's Well, after which the path turns inland, rising and falling between fields. When the grassy track reaches a crest there is a view of Ardmore Round Tower with the Comeragh Mountains beyond. The track leads to a minor road running down to Ardmore Church and the Round Tower, where the churchyard abounds in interest. Continue down the road, passing St. Paul's Church of Ireland to reach a crossroads. Left is the Round Tower Hotel. Straight on is the course of St. Declan's Way to Cashel. Right leads straight through Ardmore to return to the sea. There are places offering food, drink and accommodation along the way.

Ardmore

The Round Tower at Ardmore is one of Ireland's latest, dating from the 12th century, and one of the tallest, rising to nearly 100ft (30m). The church is known as the Cathedral. Ardmore was one of the first bishoprics in Ireland, but not for long. The church features a mixture of periods and styles, but most of it is 12th century. Some fine carved panels on the west wall clearly depict biblical scenes, again dating from the 12th century. Two ancient Ogham stones from the churchyard have been placed in the nave of the church. The smallest

A detail of Adam and Eve from the ruins at Ardmore

building in the churchyard is St. Declan's Oratory, or Beannachán, and is perhaps the most significant structure, as it was the shrine over the burial place of St. Declan. It could date from the 8th century but was remodelled and reroofed in 1716.

St. Declan

St. Declan was one of four missionaries who worked in Ireland before the arrival of St. Patrick. He may have come from south-west Britain and founded a church at Ardmore in the year 416, though the ruins seen around town date from much later. His feast day is July 24th; a time when Ardmore is already busy with holidaymakers. St. Declan's Stone is said to have floated across the sea from Wales and pilgrims would squirm through the gap underneath it in the hope of receiving a cure. St. Declan met St. Patrick, but later retired to the hermitage site which is passed on the cliff walk.

WALK 7

Great Island

Walking guidebooks invariably skip Cork Harbour, which is a pity. True, there are large, unsightly industrial areas, including dockyards, oil refineries, power stations and chemical works, and the sky is criss-crossed by pylon lines. Amazingly, much of Great Island is still pleasant rolling farmland, while Cobh is an immensely colourful and interesting little town. A circuit of Great Island is accomplished largely on roads, but there are some paths through fields and forest, as well as along the quayside.

The Route

Distance:	15½ miles (25 kilometres).
Start:	Cobh Railway Station - 794663.
Maps:	OS Discovery Sheets 81 & 87.
Terrain:	Mostly roads, with occasional paths and tracks.
Parking:	Plenty of parking around Cobh.
Transport:	Regular rail services from Cork to Cobh.

Arrive in Cobh by rail if you can, hopping from Cork city to Little Island to Fota Island and Great Island. The railway station is in the

same building as the Cobh Heritage Centre. Walking straight through the colourful town, passing the tourist information office and a small quayside park complete with cannons. St. Colman's Cathedral towers above the town and there is plenty of parking along the way.

The Town Hall is a small, colourful building on the quayside. The road climbs steeply up Harbour Row and Harbour Terrace to reach East Hill, enjoying fine views across the harbour. Avoid any cul de sacs to the right, then the road turns sharply inland. At this point, climb a flight of steps and follow a concrete path and road past some houses, then continue along a tarmac path. Turn right at the end of the path to cross a small green and reach a road junction.

Follow the road signposted for Ballymore and Marloag. The road runs downhill, with the Highland B&B to the left and a grotto to the right, reaching Cuskinny Marsh Nature Reserve at the bottom. There is a small car park beside Cuskinny Bay. Follow the road uphill between a tall wall and a wooded bank and watch for traffic. At the top, where the road broadens and swings left, turn right along a narrower road. This is well wooded in places, but there are views out to the mouth of Cork Harbour.

When a bench is reached at a junction, turn right and head down through the valley of Glenmore to reach the shore. There is a small car park and a notice reads '21 Ditches' - the name of a path leading to Marloge Wood. Follow the road at first, but leave it when it suddenly bends left uphill. Follow a track, avoiding private gateways, then use a path to cross a gorse and bramble bank. Walk through a small wood to reach a road. Turn right towards the shore, then left along a path cutting around the edge of a garden. Climb some wooded steps and descend some stone steps to reach a track near a whitewashed cottage with a corrugated roof. Walk up the track, then turn right round the top of a field to reach a farm. Keep right to follow its access road to Marloge Wood.

Enter the forest car park and leave by following a track downhill. Though the track swings right, it later swings left to continue round the island. Walk straight through a turning space and the track leads to a gate. A grassy track continues across a field to reach a road. Following this downhill leads to the East Ferry Marina and the Marlogue Inn, ideally situated for lunch. Note the little church across the East Passage. The only way around the northern corner of Great Island involves an unpleasant shingle and seaweed shore walk, so it is better to switch to roads to complete the circuit.

Follow the road away from the Marlogue Inn, turning right and right again, passing an impressive old gatehouse at Ballywalter, then turning left at the next road junction. Walk over to the northern shore of the island, where the road runs close to the water. Pass Ashgrove Lodge and the Old Coach House, noting a small, converted castle. The road continues behind a low point crowned by a Martello Tower, then passes saltings before cutting inland again. Turn right at the next signposted junction to reach the narrows of the Belvelly Channel, guarded by a stout castle near an arched bridge. Fota Island is just across Belvelly Bridge, but you need to stay on Great Island to complete the circuit.

The next stretch can be unpleasant. A busy, bendy stretch of the R624 road with no footway needs to be followed past the Irish Fertiliser plant at Marino Point. There is a bad bend beneath a railway bridge, then Carrigaloe Railway Station is reached. This offers a speedy return to Cobh, otherwise walk past Peg's Pub, now on a footway, continuing past the Passage West Ferry, Rinn Ronain Hotel and the graceful cranes of the Cork Dockyard. On entering Cobh, watch for a signpost for the Cobh Heritage Centre and use this road to return immediately to the shore. A walk along the quays looking out to Haulbowline Island leads straight back to the railway station.

Cobh

Cobh is situated on one of the great natural harbours of the world, but only really began to develop during the 18th century. During the Napoleonic wars, up to 300 ships could be counted at anchor. The Cobh Heritage Centre, housed in part of the railway station, tells all about the town. Convict ships sailed for Australia from 1791 and 'coffin' ships took emigrants to America from 1845 in the wake of the Great Famine. When Queen Victoria visited in 1849, Cobh was renamed Queenstown, but reverted to its old name in 1920. Its development as a resort has resulted in a colourful waterfront scene of tall buildings, crowned by a fine Cathedral. The quayside has a memorial to the many emigrants who embarked for the United

States, including Annie Moore, who was the first person to pass through the immigration centre on Ellis Island when it opened on 1st January 1892. Cobh was Ireland's main transatlantic port until the 1950s and it is still occasionally visited by cruise liners. There are plenty of shops, pubs, restaurants and a range of accommodation options.

Cuskinny

There are two varied habitats either side of the road at Cuskinny; a reedy pool designated as Cuskinny Marsh Nature Reserve, and a shingly shore. Some of the roadside trees are marked with their names, while a noticeboard beside the shore indicates the range of birds which might be spotted: oystercatcher, turnstone, curlew, cormorant, great northern diver, guillemot, red breasted merganser, great crested grebe, common and sandwich tern, rock pipit and gannet.

Marloag

Also written as Marloge and Marlogue, this area overlooks the East Channel. A small marina has been developed at the site of the now defunct East Ferry. Marloge Woods offer quiet walking and the nearby '21 Ditches' path indeed crosses a total of twenty-one field boundaries. The Marlogue Inn is the only place offering food and drink on this side of Great Island.

Cork Harbour

Cork Harbour is a splendid sheltered harbour criss-crossed by deep navigable channels. Cork city was itself founded on an island bounded by tidal channels and there are plenty more islands found by a study of the map. Great Island is the largest, followed by Little Island, which is heavily industrialised. Between the two is the wooded Fota Island, where an interesting wildlife park has been established. Other notable islands include Haulbowline Island, home to an important naval base; Spike Island, with a prison in an old fort; and Corkbeg Island, which is occupied by an oil refinery. One of the finest ways to view Cork Harbour and the Cobh waterfront is from the Swansea Cork Ferry.

WALK 8

Sherkin Island

Regular ferries ply between Baltimore and Sherkin Island, making this a popular choice among islands. While most of the island is low-lying and access is mostly along roads, there is a high crest which is quite rugged, offering a tough little walk with extensive views and fine cliffs. Be warned that this high crest is spiky with gorse scrub and paths are quite vague. It is easy to stray off course in places and some areas may prove impassable with thorny scrub. The substantial ruins of Sherkin Abbey dominate the usual approach to the island.

The Route

Distance:	5 miles (8 kilometres).
Start:	Sherkin Abbey - 029257.
Map:	OS Discovery Sheet 88.
Terrain:	Road walking, followed by rugged walking over gorse scrub.
Parking:	Cars cannot be taken onto the island. Parking is available around Baltimore.
Transport:	Bus Eireann table number 251 serves Baltimore. There are regular daily ferry services to Sherkin Island from Baltimore.

Sherkin Abbey is seen immediately above the pier

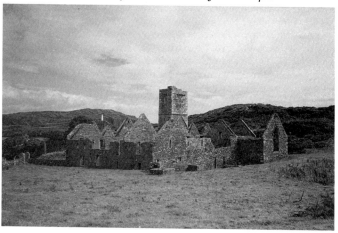

41

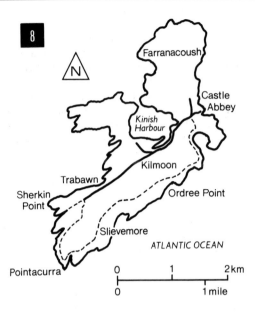

8

Farranacoush

Castle Abbey

Kinish Harbour

Kilmoon

Trabawn

Sherkin Point

Ordree Point

Slievemore

ATLANTIC OCEAN

Pointacurra

0   1   2 km

0   1 mile

The little harbour on Sherkin Island is dominated by the ruins of Sherkin Abbey. Follow the road up past the Abbey, passing a telephone box and the Abbey Store. Access to the coast is quite limited, so it is as well to walk all the way across the island by road. Sherkin Library is passed on the shores of Kinish Harbour, then the road rises and passes the Roman Catholic church, overlooking Trabawn Strand. Follow the road onwards, turning left and right as it becomes a stony track. The last few houses on the island are passed, but don't walk all the way to the very last house.

Turn left off the track before the last house and follow a narrow path which can be a bit muddy as it rises towards the cliffs at the south-western end of Sherkin Island. The cliffs have shattered faces and rise above Gascanane Sound, facing Clear Island. Swing left and climb further uphill to reach the rugged top of Slievemore, crossing gorse, rock and heather. Views stretch around to include Clear Island, Mizen Head, parts of the Sheep's Head and Beara Peninsula, as well as many fine heights in West Cork. Baltimore and its nearest headlands are also in view.

Follow a low stone wall over Slievemore and keep to the rugged crest. The gorse scrub can be abrasive and paths are quite vague. Go through a little gateway in the wall later. There is a view over a rocky inlet, while a few houses can be seen across a broad gap. Keep well above the inlet, but also keep to the right of the houses, still aiming to walk along the rugged crest of the island. Eventually, there are more little walls and fences to cross, and a small lighthouse can be seen in the distance. What can't be seen for a while is the inlet known as Horseshoe Harbour. As this is approached, the ground becomes quite rough and walking becomes more difficult.

Turning around Horseshoe Harbour, look carefully for a path, which links with a clearer path, running past a handful of houses above the bay. A track leads to a crossroads near the Abbey Store, where a decision needs to be made. If time is pressing and a ferry is due, then turn right for the pier. If there is time to spare, then head straight through the crossroads to reach the Jolly Roger Tavern, Murphy's Bar and the Islander Restaurant.

Sherkin Abbey
This is actually a Franciscan Friary, founded in 1460 by the O'Driscolls. Although the ruins are substantial and include domestic additions, the place enjoyed only a brief life and was destroyed in 1537. Raiders from Waterford fired the abbey and destroyed most of the buildings on the island. The O'Driscolls inhabited the nearby Dun-na-Long Castle, which was seized for a time during the raid. The castle can be reached by walking a short way down a track from Murphy's Bar and the Islander Restaurant.

Baltimore
A peaceful fishing village, where ferries operate to a spread of islands, but in the summer and at weekends it can be busy. In 1631 the place was raided by Algerian pirates, who slaughtered most of the inhabitants and carried around 200 people into slavery in North Africa. This event was known as the Sack of Baltimore. The village has given its name to Baltimore in the USA, and a study of the map will reveal that there is a Long Island nearby too!

WALK 9

Cape Clear Island

Cape Clear Island is the most southerly of Ireland's islands, with Cape Clear generally regarded as the most southerly point. Even further south, however, is the notorious Fastnet Rock, easily identified by its lighthouse. There are some interesting rocky points on Cape Clear Island, some fine cliffs, good coastal views and enough paths, tracks and roads to allow an interesting exploration. Ferries run all year to and from Baltimore, with summer services from Schull. Ferries moor at the North Harbour, and while facilities around the island are good, they are also rather scattered.

The Route

Distance:	12 miles (19 kilometres).
Start:	North Harbour - 955219.
Map:	OS Discovery Sheet 88.
Terrain:	Roads, tracks and paths, with some stretches being pathless.
Parking:	Cars cannot be taken onto the island. There are plenty of parking places around Baltimore and Schull.
Transport:	Bus Eireann table number 251 serves Baltimore and table number 46 serves Schull.There are ferry services from Baltimore throughout the year, with further services from Schull during the summer.

There are all sorts of features of interest around North Harbour on the island. A ruined church and holy well are dedicated to St Ciarán, while there is also a shop, information office and telephone. Turn left to leave the harbour, following a road steeply uphill past a pub called the Nightjar. Cross a gap and descend past Ciarán Danny Mike's Bar. The An Oige Youth Hostel and Adventure Centre is at the bottom of the road beside South Harbour. Pass in front of the building, then follow the road uphill. Turn right up a track to Glen West. The track leads to the 'Most Southerly House', but turn right as signposted 'Hikers' and follow a narrow path onwards. Walk

The amazing rock arch on Cape Clear Island

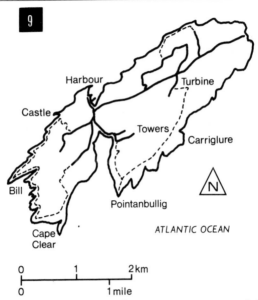

9

Harbour

Turbine

Castle

Towers

Carriglure

Bill

Pointanbullig

Cape Clear

N

ATLANTIC OCEAN

| 0 | 1 | 2 km |
| 0 | | 1 mile |

across gorse scrub and bracken, then out onto a grassy point where there is impressive cliff scenery. Fulmars may be observed soaring around these cliffs. Adventurous walkers could aim for the rocky end of Pointanbullig. Even better, there is a rock arch which is crossed on the way, and when the tide is low it is possible, with great care, to walk through from one side to the other. Barnacle encrusted rocks offer a fairly good grip and seals might be spotted in the water.

Retrace steps uphill from Pointanbullig and turn right to walk along the high, rugged crest of the island. Walk overlooking the sea, with twin stone towers ahead, and keep to the seaward side of a low drystone wall. A couple of fences need to be crossed, with gorse scrub, heather, bracken and grass underfoot. There are narrow paths, but these can be vague in places. The twin towers stand in one enclosure. A round lighthouse tower of dressed granite stands alongside an older, square, signal tower. Keep to the right to pass the towers, then continue along the high crest, still linking vague paths and crossing low stone walls. Aim for the wind turbines on the highest part of the island at 525ft (160m). There is a gate, trig point and cairn on top of the hill. Views take in the whole of Cape Clear Island, Fastnet Rock, Mizen Head, Sheep's Head, Hungry Hill, other hills in West Cork, Sherkin Island and nearby headlands.

Follow a grassy track down from the turbines and turn right to follow a narrow road downhill. At a crossroads in the middle of the island the route could be adapted in a number of ways, but here are a series of directions to let you make the most of the place. First, turn right and follow the road all the way to a small slipway at the north-eastern end of the island. Next, turn around and retrace steps uphill, turning right along a narrow road which runs back down towards the northern coast of the island. A grassy track runs onwards from the end of the road. Turn left at the end, following a rugged strip of ground which later features a narrow path. Take care, as the cliffs are rather crumbly and in places the path is very near the edge. It may sometimes be necessary to walk through one of the fields alongside. After passing a small fish-farm, look for a grassy track climbing uphill and follow it to a road. Turn right to follow the road uphill, turning right at a higher junction to pass St. Ciarán's Roman Catholic Church and a Heritage Centre. The road runs gradually downhill, then falls more steeply to a junction passed earlier in the day.

Turn left up the road, then turn right and right again as signposted for O'Reagan's B&B on Lake Road. At the top of the road, turn right at a gate and follow a stony track which winds uphill, then downhill towards the ruined Dunamore Castle; a former O'Driscoll stronghold. Don't go all the way down to the castle, but turn left to start tracing the cliff-line around the island. There is little space to manoeuvre between the fields and the cliff edges, so stay inside the fields at first. Some of the fields are bounded by low stone walls, while others have electric fences which need to be crossed with care. Pass the mouth of little Lough Errul, then there is later a more rugged point which can be followed to its end at the Bill of Cape Clear.

There is some gorse scrub on the rest of the rugged headlands, with only vague paths to follow. An occasional fence might need to be crossed while turning around the heads of some rugged ravines. It's also possible to short-cut behind the headlands, though this means missing some of the fine cliff scenery. Be sure to have a look at the rocky point of Cape Clear, even if you don't fancy tackling an exposed scramble along its crest! This point is notable for its bird-life and can sometimes be quite busy with bird-watchers. From some viewpoints it is possible to see a hole through this rocky ridge, and it is certainly possible to look across the mouth of South Harbour to the rock arch at the end of Pointanbullig.

Follow a more obvious path onwards along the top of the rugged slope, in view of the cairn on the summit of Firbreaga. The path runs through a gap in a wall, continuing through a couple of fields to join a track. The track passes a farm and a road runs onwards. After passing a few more buildings, fields and a campsite, turn left on a gap beside Ciarán Danny Mike's Bar to follow the road back down to North Harbour.

St. Ciarán of Cape Clear Island

There were four notable people who brought Christianity to Ireland before the arrival of St. Patrick. St. Ciarán was reputed to have been the first; a native of Cape Clear Island, who was born in the 4th century and heard about Christianity from passing seafarers. He resolved to find out more by leaving the island to study in Rome, returning some time later to found a monastic settlement. Ciarán is therefore the patron saint of the island and there is a ruined church and holy well dedicated to him on the North Harbour. His birthplace is pointed out on the road up towards the Roman Catholic church. The island's Heritage Centre is located in an old National School and contains a wealth of information.

WALK 10

Mizen Head

Mizen Head is signposted as 'The Most South Westerly Point in Ireland'. Sitting on the end of the point is the Mizen Vision Centre, which is contained within a series of former lighthouse buildings. While payment is required, and the route is really very short, the place is certainly worth visiting and has tremendous cliff scenery. A famous, picturesque, white concrete bridge allows access to the lighthouse buildings, while the Mizen Vision exhibition deals with the natural history of the area and the history and development of the Irish lighthouse system.

The Route

Distance:	½ mile (1 kilometre).
Start:	Mizen Head - 739236.
Map:	OS Discovery Sheet 88.
Terrain:	Well-surfaced paths and steps with ample safety fencing.
Parking:	At the end of the road at Mizen Head.
Transport:	Bus Eireann table number 46 runs only to Goleen.

This is a short and simple walk, with route directions hardly being necessary. Park at the end of the road to Mizen Head, and pay at the snacks cabin for access to the Mizen Vision Centre. The path is enclosed in stout safety fencing, with zig-zags and steps leading to an arched concrete bridge spanning a rocky chasm. There are fine views of the cliffs from the bridge, beyond which are the former lighthouse buildings. Exhibitions cover the coastline, lighthouses, wrecks, seabirds, etc. The last few steps and walkways lead onto a final stance allowing fine views. After exploring the centre and enjoying the views, retrace steps to the car park.

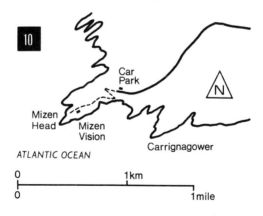

WALK 11

Sheep's Head

The Sheep's Head is a long and narrow peninsula which is entirely encircled by the waymarked Sheep's Head Way. The very end of the peninsula offers a fine cliff coast walk, featuring a ruined village and copper mines, rugged scenery and extensive views. A little lighthouse sits on the end of the headland, while the highest point gained bears the ruins of an old signal tower. The route takes in a series of old tracks over low hills, then cuts across the peninsula by road, before following a cliff path back towards the lighthouse, turning the end of the point to complete the circuit. Most of the route is marked as the Sheep's Head Way.

The Route

Distance:	12 miles (20 kilometres).
Start:	The 'Turning Table' at Tooreen - 733341.
Map:	OS Discovery Sheet 88
Terrain:	Rugged paths and tracks, which can be boggy in places.
Parking:	At the 'Turning Table' at Tooreen near the end of the road.
Transport:	Bus Eireann table number 255 serves Kilcrohane on Saturdays only.

Motorists who drive nearly all the way to the end of the Sheep's Head can park at a place known as the 'Turning Table' before the last farm buildings at Tooreen. There is an information board about the Sheep's Head Way and there may be snacks available in the summer months. Most visitors head straight for the lighthouse, but this walk makes a long circuit before reaching the lighthouse towards the end of the walk.

Follow the path marked behind the information board, crossing a stile over a fence, climbing uphill, then crossing another stile. Walk up to an old lookout building and cross another stile. A rocky spine leads to a trig point at 795ft (239m). Views take in the Sheep's Head, Mizen Head, Dursey Head, the mountains of the Beara Peninsula, and the inlets of Bantry Bay and Dunmanus Bay. Continue along the rocky spine, passing a ruined signal tower. A grassy track with a fence alongside leads downhill, becoming rather more clear after crossing a stile. The track passes a couple of houses and an access road leads down to a minor road.

Turn left along the road, then right to cross a stile. A rugged moorland slope is crossed by a broad, grassy track which can be boggy in places. Look out for waymark posts and cross two stiles over fences along the way. The path becomes narrower and is flanked by gorse. Cross another stile and follow a path past a house. A marker points to the right, where a stile is crossed, then the route runs down to a road. Turn left along the road, but walk straight onwards when the Sheep's Head Way turns right. At the next junction, turn left, following the road uphill, keeping to the right, then downhill, still keeping to the right. Climb over a little gap at Clash, then look out for a stile and gateway to the left. While some walkers might have spotted an opportunity to short-cut at Eskraha, the area around Gortavallig is too good to miss!

Follow a grassy track gently downhill from the gateway, but look for another, more rugged path off to the left. This path leads past a series of ruined buildings known as the 'Crimea'. Further along, an old copper mining area is passed at Gortavallig. A steep

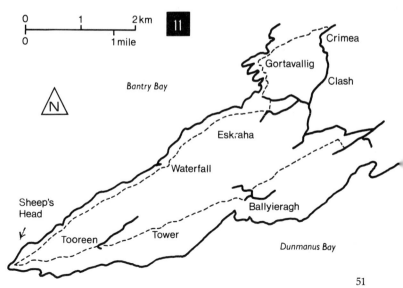

cliff and a narrow path features a rope which more cautious walkers might like to hold for security. A row of old mine buildings are passed, then the route becomes a roller-coaster as it proceeds, crossing rocky ridges and little valleys. What appears to be a blow-hole along the way was actually excavated by a farmer who hoped that the sea would throw out sand and seaweed in times of storm, to be used to improve the land! The waymarked route leads to a track near the bouldery beach.

Turn left up the track to leave the beach, then turn right up a narrow, walled, grassy track. When a road is reached at the top, turn right along a track, crossing stiles beside gates as the track rises and draws closer to the sea. The track gives way to a boggy path over a broad moorland rise around Eskraha, where there are only a handful of scattered houses in view. The path drifts downhill and crosses a stile, passing a waterfall and rocky inlet. Climb uphill again, following marker posts along a kind of grassy trough flanked by rockier slopes. At times the path runs fairly close to the cliff edges and there are signs warning of this from time to time. Looking ahead, an electricity transmission line can be seen and this indicates that the Sheep's Head Lighthouse is close to hand. The lighthouse is actually quite small, and is seated against the rocky headland.

Follow a well-trodden path inland from the Sheep's Head, passing the little Lough Akeen and generally climbing uphill. The path is braided in places, but all the paths return to the car park at the 'Turning Table' at Tooreen.

The 'Crimea'

The sad stone cottage ruins encountered on this walk are referred to locally as the 'Crimea' and were abandoned by the 1940s. The nick-name was derived from the constant bickering among the families who lived there, prompting one visitor to liken the place to the Crimea, which was at war at the time!

Gortavallig

The old copper mines at Gortavallig have counterparts on the Beara and Mizen peninsulas, as all the headlands are streaked with copper ores. Unlike the mines on the neighbouring peninsulas, Gortavallig had a very short life and only one shipment of ore was ever dispatched. The visible workings include a number of shafts, a pool of water for power and a row of ruined cottages. The man behind the venture was a Cornishman and Cornish labour was employed at the mine.

Sheep's Head Way
The Sheep's Head Way is easily one of the best waymarked trails in Ireland, completely encircling the Sheep's Head Peninsula. The route starts and finishes in Bantry, and makes the most of the rugged ridge along the spine of the peninsula, then takes in the cliffs described above, ending with more gentle countryside, linking a series of little villages. The route measures 55 miles (88 kilometres).

WALK 12
Bere Island

Bere Island sits in Bantry Bay close to Castletownbere. There are two ferries giving regular daily access, and the waymarked Beara Way offers a couple of scenic loops exploring the roads, hills and coast. You could complete the entire waymarked trail, which stretches the full length of the island, but includes quite a lot of road-walking. Alternatively, you could limit the road-walking and head for the hills and coast in a loop around the western end of the island. Both options are included in the route description, based on the ferry from Castletownbere.

The Route

Distance:	8 miles (13 kilometres) or 17^{1}/$_{2}$ miles (28 kilometres).
Start:	At the western ferry slip on Bere Island - 686446.
Map:	OS Discovery Sheet 84.
Terrain:	A variety of waymarked roads, tracks and paths. Some western parts can be rocky and boggy.
Parking:	Cars can be taken onto Bere Island, but it is best to leave them at the harbour at Castletownbere.
Transport:	Bus Eireann table number 46 serves Castletownbere in summer and at weekends. Ferries serve the western end of the Bere Island, while the village of Rerrin also has a ferry.

The route described around Bere Island is based on the waymarked Bere Island Walk, which is part of the Beara Way. Start by walking along roads as described, then decide whether to complete only the western loop, over the hills and around the coast, or the entire circuit of the island. There are two ferries to Bere Island; one from the harbour at Castletownbere and the other from Pontoon to Rerrin. The route below is described from Castletownbere.

Step ashore on Bere Island and follow the road uphill from the pier, through Derrycreeveen. Turn left along the Beara Way as signposted for Rerrin, over a rise and along a narrow road. The road passes Harbour View B&B and a school at Ballyinakilla. Follow the road uphill and enjoy the view across Bere Haven to the mountains of the Beara Peninsula, then pass a pub and shop. Keep straight on along the road, avoiding all roads off to the left. Eventually, there is a road to the right, where there is a three-fingered signpost for the Beara Way - and a choice of routes. Decide whether you want to complete the long or short walk:

Long Walk

Follow the road straight onwards for Rerrin, rising towards a hill which is crowned with a stout Martello Tower. The road cuts across the rugged moorland slopes, with views to both sides for a while. The road runs downhill, with a left and right turn at the bottom continuing towards Rerrin. After passing close to Delmar House there is a lovely view across an inlet with the village of Rerrin beyond. There are places offering food and drink if required.

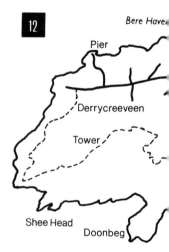

Turn left to leave Rerrin, walking alongside the harbour, then follow a road forking uphill to the right, passing a restaurant. After a bendy stretch, the road passes some army barracks. The road ends at an old gunnery, and although there is no access to Lonehort Point, there are good views along the coast and across to the mountains.

Hungry Hill looks particularly rugged. Keep right to follow a track flanked by gorse, then keep left along another track. An attractive inlet is passed at Lonehort Harbour, where the Vikings are believed to have run a trans-shipment operation. A road leads gently downhill and passes a fine wedge grave made of huge slabs of rock. The road runs fairly close to the coast, and a grassy track to the left leads to the shore. A right turn across stiles leads to a little slipway beside a couple of houses. Walking inland, a left turn up a track and path leads onto a little summit crowned by a Martello Tower, though steps need to be retraced afterwards. A right and left turn along a road and track, however, leads back to a road just outside Rerrin, where a left turn leads westwards and uphill to return to the three-fingered Beara Way signpost passed earlier in the day.

Short Walk
At the signposted road junction, walk uphill as marked for the Standing Stone. The stone is actually off to the left on a high gap, but the route crosses a stile beside a gate and follows a track further uphill. A prominent Holy Year Cross can be seen off to the right, and can be approached using a muddy path to the right. Staying on the track, however, leads across a rugged gap on Knockanallig, then downhill in a series of bends beside some rocky outcrops. At a

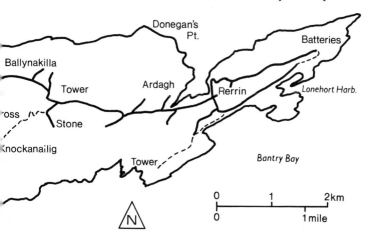

junction of tracks, turn right and climb gently uphill, then on the descent from a gap, look out for a marker pointing to the left. Walk alongside a wall and fence, crossing a boggy patch, to reach another stony track. Turn left uphill, then right up a lesser track to reach a ruined signal tower on top of a hill. Enjoy the fine views, which embrace the end of Dursey Island, the mountains of the Beara Peninsula, the hills and point of the Sheep's Head, as well as Mizen Head.

Walk along the rugged, rocky crest of the hill, keeping left of a fenced pool and side-stepping any boggy patches. Although a grassy path is reached, don't follow it for any distance, but look for more marker posts showing the way further downhill. An attractive lighthouse stands on Ardnakinna Point, and the Beara Way turns right just before reaching it. Follow a broad, grassy track which has been cut from solid rock in some places and stoutly buttressed in other places. The track later zig-zags down to the sea, so watch for a lesser path on the right, which is waymarked further across the rugged slopes. This path features stone steps and is well marked. After passing a ruin on a rougher path, join a grassy track and follow it by crossing a couple of stiles beside gates. A few houses are passed later, then at another gate, turn right along a road. A left turn along another road finally leads back to the ferry for Castletownbere.

Naval History

According to folklore, Lonehort Harbour was a Viking harbour, and recent archaeological discoveries tend to confirm this view. The harbour at Castletownbere was heavily fortified and developed by the British. They crowned four of the surrounding hills with Martello Towers, two of which survive, along with a number of barracks and other buildings. Heavy guns were mounted on some of the headlands. All the British fortifications and barracks were finally handed over to the Irish government in 1938.

WALK 13

Dursey Island

Lying off the end of the rugged Beara Peninsula, Dursey Island features a long, high crest. Access is by cablecar, offering a novel approach to the island and the walk. The walk is fully waymarked as part of the Beara Way. The route follows a track and path to the end of the island, linking the few inhabited farmhouses on the way. The return route is partly along the rugged moorland crest of the island, passing only a ruined signal tower and a couple of farmhouses. There is no accommodation on the island, but there are a handful of B&Bs on the road approaching the cablecar.

The Route

Distance:	8¹/₂ miles (14 kilometres).
Start:	Dursey Sound - 507419.
Map:	OS Discovery Sheet 84.
Terrain:	Road, tracks and vague paths run across the island.
Parking:	Cars cannot be taken onto the island. Park near the cablecar at Dursey Sound.
Transport:	There are no buses running beyond Castletownbere. Dursey Island is reached by a cablecar service which runs several times daily.

Riding a cablecar across the surging sea has to be the most unusual way to approach any of the coastal walks in this guidebook. There is a car park and toilets where the cablecar departs, while a Beara Way signpost points across Dursey Sound to Dursey Island and includes destinations such as New York and Moscow. The little wooden box passes through two pylons high above the sea and links with a road-end on Dursey Island. A few fishermen's huts can be seen off to the left, where there is also a small pier and a few small boats. As the road is followed onwards, the ruins of an old church and a graveyard lie to the left, as well as the little island of Illanebeg.

The road turns a corner and a few farmsteads can be seen across a broad dip. A track continues across another broad dip to another cluster of farms, where there is also a telephone. The track reaches

A unique cablecar ride leads across to Dursey Island

a gate, then a few fields are passed before a junction of tracks is reached. Turn left, passing above the fields and going through another gate. The track is a fine, grassy ribbon, cutting across a steep, rugged slope high above the sea. Amazingly, there is a sudden view of yet another farming landscape of fields and houses, but many are empty and derelict. Follow the track to the last farm, then continue over a hump of short heather and bracken, following the line of a fence. Cross the fence at a corner, then cross a gap where the grass is very short. A final grassy hump gives way to the end of the island, where a stout, walled enclosure can be studied. Offshore is a small tower on a rocky islet called

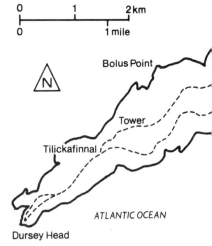

58

The Calf. Two other rocky islands can be seen; one called The Cow and the one crowned with a lighthouse called The Bull. The Skellig Rocks are more distant. Valentia Island merges with the mainland, where MacGillycuddy's Reeks and other mountains can be distinguished. Beara, the Sheep's Head and Mizen Head peninsulas are all seen in turn.

You can wander at will around the end of Dursey Island and explore the shattered, slabby cliffs. Afterwards, retrace steps over the hump of heather and bracken to reach the farm track. Walk along the track, but look out to the left to spot a waymarked path climbing up towards a prominent hilltop signal tower. The ground cover includes short heather and spiky, bulbous cushions of gorse. There is a trig point beside the ruined signal tower at 832ft (252m). Views are confined to the extreme south-west of Ireland, but are remarkably interesting.

To descend, follow a path along the crest of the island, crossing a stile over a fence, then walking down a grassy, stony track through short heather. The track drifts down to the right off a gap, but waymark posts can be seen climbing uphill with only a vague path alongside. After crossing a moorland rise, a few farm buildings will be seen off to the right, with fields rising up towards the rugged

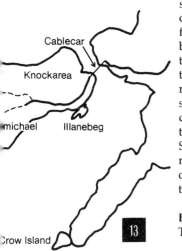

slope. Keep to the left of the fields, crossing a stile over a fence, then follow a path alongside the outer field boundaries and link with a clearer track. The track turns right and goes through a gate, rejoining the island road at a few farms. Turn left and simply follow the road across a broad dip, around a corner, passing above the old graveyard, to return to Dursey Sound and the cablecar. You might notice that the cablecar contains a copy of Psalm 91, with an instruction to 'read every day for protection.'

Beara Way
The walk around Dursey Island is

based on the waymarked Beara Way. This route completely encircles the Beara Peninsula, visiting Dursey Island by way of a spur from the village of Allihies. The route takes in plenty of rugged hillsides, as well as stretches of coast and quiet roads. There are plenty of archaeological sites along the way, which have been signposted to catch the attention of walkers. The walk around Bere Island is also part of the Beara Way. The total distance of the route is 125 miles (200 kilometres).

WALK 14

Derrynane Bay

A short coastal walk can be enjoyed in the Derrynane National Historic Park near Caherdaniel. The park is centred on the home of Daniel O'Connell 'The Liberator'. The park is mostly wooded, but there is a belt of sand dunes around Derrynane Bay, as well as access to Abbey Island when the tide is out. The walk is quite short and simple, but abounds in interest, as the grounds and gardens of Derrynane House can be explored as well as the coast.

The Route

Distance:	3 miles (5 kilometres).
Start:	Derrynane House, Caherdaniel - 529588.
Maps:	OS Discovery Sheets 83 or 84.
Terrain:	A short, easy circuit on roads and dune paths.
Parking:	At Derrynane House.
Transport:	Bus Eireann table number 280 offers a summer service to Caherdaniel.

Derrynane House is signposted from the village of Caherdaniel off the scenic Ring of Kerry road. There is ample parking and even if walkers arrive by bus, Derrynane House is only a short walk from Caherdaniel. The house is the centre of the Derrynane National Historic Park, and was formerly the home of Daniel O'Connell, popularly known as 'The Liberator'. It's worth having a good look around the house, chapel and gardens before progressing onto a short coastal walk around Derrynane Bay.

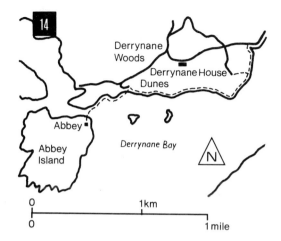

Follow the narrow road away from Derrynane House as if returning to Caherdaniel. A sign on the right points to a nature trail and toilets, though a little further along the road, another signpost points right to a tall Ogham stone. If the tide is out, and if a nearby river is running low, it is possible to start walking around Derrynane Bay simply by heading for the sandy shore and turning right. If the tide is in, or if the river is high, then backtrack along the road and take the turning signposted for the nature trail. After walking past a lagoon in a wooded area, continue through a car park and follow a path signposted for the Derrynane Dunes Nature Trail. If this second option is chosen, turn left when emerging from the woods, then turn right along the coast. An area of grassland is parcelled by fencing, but there are stiles.

Either way, narrow paths around Derrynane Bay can be followed. Short grass gives way to longer and tougher marram grass, and there are generally paths fairly close to the shore. In fact, some walkers may prefer to follow the sandy shore, although there are rounded humps of rock further along. Views are restricted to an arc around the bay, taking in a couple of small islands. The coastal walk is fairly short, but if the tide is out, then it is worth extending it as far as the ruined Derrynane Abbey on Abbey Island. Many members of the O'Connell family are buried here.

You need to backtrack from Abbey Island to reach a car park and a narrow road. A left turn up the road leads to Keatings Bar, while a right turn leads through woods to a couple of gateways on the right. The second gateway is marked as an entrance to Derrynane House, bringing the walk to a close.

Derrynane National Historic Park

The woodlands and coast around Derrynane House have been a National Historic Park since being acquired by the State in 1966. Derrynane House was the ancestral home of Daniel O'Connell; lawyer, politician and statesman. His major campaign was to have the harsh penal laws repealed, earning him the title of 'The Liberator'. This was acheived in 1829. Another major campaign was for the repeal of the Act of Union, though ill-health and the Great Famine saw this grind to a halt late in the middle of the 19th century. Derrynane House, built by O'Connell, replaced an earlier house also used by the family and has a number of O'Connell's possessions and furnishings. An audio-visual theatre offers a quick overview of his life and achievements. There is a tea room, while the surrounding gardens and woodlands feature a network of paths. Nature trail booklets for use around the dunes are also available.

WALK 15

Valentia Island

Valentia Island is often described as being sub-tropical, and while it may be luxuriantly vegetated in places, other parts are rather exposed and feature only short grass and heather. The most exposed part of the island is surely Bray Head, which can be approached using a track to an old signal tower. There are opportunities to complete a longer loop, maybe even starting from the interesting Skellig Experience Visitor Centre at Portmagee. Some fine cliffs can be explored, then while cutting inland there is a chance to study St. Brendan's Well.

The Route

Distance:	8¹/₂ miles (14 kilometres).
Start:	Skellig Centre near Portmagee - 371735.
Map:	OS Discovery Sheet 83.
Terrain:	Some good paths, tracks and roads, but also pathless stretches.
Parking:	At the Skellig Centre or on the road to Bray Tower.
Transport:	There are no bus services nearer than Cahersiveen. Although there is a ferry service from Reenard Point near Cahersiveen to Knightstown on Valentia Island, there is also a bridge onto the island from Portmagee.

While cars can be parked on the approach to Bray Head on Valentia Island, this walk is structured to start and finish at the Skellig Experience Visitor Centre at Portmagee. You will be able to see the distant Skelligs from this walk and the centre offers the chance to study their history and heritage beforehand. There may also be

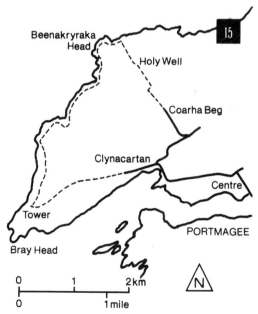

cruises out to the rocks.

Leave the Skellig Centre by following the road uphill and turn left. Take another road left which is signposted for Bray Tower. There is a parking space along this road if a shorter walk is required. Follow a track uphill and cross a stile beside a gate. There is a fine view across the inlet separating Valentia Island from the mainland. The Skelligs should be in view if the weather is clear. A solitary telegraph pole stands higher up the track, which ends at an old signal tower in a walled enclosure. Enjoy the views over the cliffs, as well as taking note of the abundance of seabirds.

Turn right to follow a path along the cliffs, overlooking a prominent rock stack. Look back towards the old signal tower and beyond to the sharp end of Bray Head. Walk over a dome of grass and heather at 793ft (239m), then pick a way carefully downhill and follow the line of a fence close to the cliff edge. Wild goats might be seen on the rugged slopes. Cross a stile and continue following the fence, looking over the cliffs at more rock stacks. An eroded gully cuts inland and needs to be turned. There are fence junctions here, along with another stile.

Walk further around the cliffs, which are unfenced, while a boggy moorland with turf cuttings stretches inland. The ground becomes grassier and there are traces of old field boundaries. The cliff scenery is dramatic in places and seals may be spotted. When a more substantial wall and fence are reached, walk alongside to head inland. The ground can be rather wet and you may prefer to walk along a nearby turf bank for a firmer footing. St. Brendan's Well and a handful of old stone crosses are reached, then a track crosses a bridge over a river and leads further inland. Three farmhouses are passed, then the track rises to another group of buildings. Turn right along a minor road, which later descends and passes the Old School House before reaching a signposted junction. Bray Tower is signposted off to the right, if you have parked a car along that road, otherwise turn left to complete the walk. A right turn further along leads back to the Skellig Centre and the bridge off the island to Portmagee.

Skellig Experience Visitor Centre
Skellig Michael and the Little Skellig are two amazing, rugged,

tussocky and squelchy away from the summit, then becomes steeper and rougher, featuring rock and heather. There is no real path, but a prominent drystone wall can be followed straight downhill, offering the easiest line on the rugged slope. When a gate and a Dingle Way marker post are reached at the bottom, don't go through, but turn right instead.

Walk uphill and follow a broad, grassy strip alongside another drystone wall. Bright yellow paint has been applied to posts and rocks to indicate the course of the Dingle Way throughout, so there should be no problems with route-finding. The path rises, then descends gently, becoming narrower on a rugged slope. The path rises to cross a stream in a little valley, before descending above a couple of farm buildings. Note the stone 'clochán' beehive huts above the buildings, as well as scattered cairns formed after clearing stones from the slope to make small fields. As the path is followed onwards, look out for other 'clochán' sites in the lower fields. The drystone wall rises and there are no signs of habitations for a while, then after crossing a stile the path is marked by a series of posts leading down to the Slea Head road. There are fine views of the Blasket Islands.

Turn right to follow the road past a group of houses which include the Enchanted Forest Fairytale Museum and Bear Cafe, as well as the Slea Head Farm B&B. A road to the left leads into a car park, from where a short path can be followed onto the dome of Dunmore Head, overlooking the Blasket Islands. This is a worthwhile detour, and the site is notable for being the burial place of Bishop Erc in AD 512. Follow the road onwards, passing a graveyard, then turn left as signposted 'Ferry to the Great Blasket Island'. There is a small car park and the way to the ferry lies off to the left. Keep straight along the road, however, following it down to a bend, then dropping straight down to cross a valley. The short climb uphill leads straight back to the Great Blasket Visitor Centre.

'Clochán' Sites

The southern slopes of Slea Head feature numerous stone 'clochán' beehive huts. There is no direct access to them from the course of the Dingle Way, but some of them can be visited from the road around Slea Head. Some stand singly, while others are arranged in twos

Stone 'clochán' beehive huts are found round Slea Head

and threes, maybe within a larger enclosure. They are reputed to have been inhabited by hermits and monks, and certainly the countryside around Dingle is rich in ancient Christian remains. Others believe that the huts could be as much as 2,000 years old.

Great Blasket Visitor Centre
The Great Blasket Island was evacuated in 1953, but not before several of the islanders had written accounts of their lives, customs and traditions. The visitor centre is a long, sloping building with audio-visual facilities and panels featuring several of the islanders, focusing on their literary works. Some of the exhibits concentrate on the austere lives of the last inhabitants, and there are also notes on the current state of the Irish language.

WALK 17

Great Blasket Island

It is almost unheard of for anyone to overwinter on the Great Blasket Island, though a couple of houses have been rescued from the ruins of a deserted village and these are inhabited during the summer months. Contrast the scene today with the scenes described by several of the island inhabitants in the early 20th century. The island was evacuated in 1953 but a wealth of literature describes the everyday life and work of the people. Ferries run in the summer and there may be food and drink available. Paths allow the whole length of the island to be explored and views in clear weather are superb.

The Route

Distance:	8¹/₂ miles (14 kilometres).
Start:	The Village, Great Blasket Island - 283976.
Map:	OS Discovery Sheet 70.
Terrain:	Mostly grassy tracks and paths, but vague in the west.
Parking:	On the mainland above Dunquin Pier.
Transport:	Bus Eireann table numbers 276 & 281 serve Dunquin. Ferries run to the Great Blasket in the summer months from the pier at Dunquin.

This walk really starts on the mainland, twisting and turning down a steep, zigzag concrete path to a stout pier. The sea is spiked with rocky stacks and the ferry plies across the Blasket Sound to reach the Great Blasket Island. The actual landing requires a smaller boat, then you climb up a rocky ramp and continue along a delightful track of short grass. Ahead are the ruins of the village, and only a mere handful of buildings have been restored. A left turn uphill leads towards a seasonal craft shop, but turn right to walk away from it up another fine, grassy track. A right turn later leads to a seasonal café, but branch to the left up another grassy track and pass high above the building, leaving the village behind.

The grassy track rises and turns a corner, revealing a steep slope of grass, heather and in summer a variety of flowers. Although most of the way is firm and dry, there may be a few soft and wet patches. The track rises gently, cutting across the steep northern slopes of the

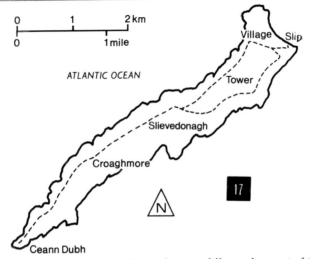

Great Blasket, and eventually reaches a saddle on the crest of the island. A junction of grassy tracks here is known as the 'Traffic Lights'. Keep walking upwards and onwards, passing a stony shoulder where a couple of ring forts can be distinguished. The path is narrow, following the very crest of the island, crossing a heathery summit called Slievedonagh at 937ft (281m).

Keep walking across a broad gap, where the path is flanked by bracken, to reach the slightly higher summit of Croaghmore at 961ft (292m). Along the way, note the steep and rocky slopes falling down to the right. Some call this the Fatal Cliff, others call it the Sorrowful Slope. There is a trig point on Croaghmore, and in clear weather a most extensive view can be enjoyed. The other Blasket Islands are in sight; Inishvickillane, Inishnabro, Tearaght and Inishtooskert. Sybil Head and the Three Sisters give way to the whole of Brandon Mountain, Eagle Mountain, Slea Head and Dingle Bay. MacGillycuddy's Reeks and other heights on the Iveragh Peninsula lead the eye to Valentia Island, with a glimpse of the Beara Peninsula beyond. Out to sea are the remote Skelligs.

There is no real path onwards to the end of the island, and at first the descent is on rushy, boggy ground. Shorter grass and patches of heather are crossed and there is a conspicuous circular drystone enclosure surrounded by abundant thrift. There is a heathery spread before a final drop to a saddle, where blocky rocks are exposed around Ceann Dubh at the very end of the island. This is usually as close as anyone gets to Inishvickillane, Inishnabro, and the pyramidal form of Tearaght; the last, battered remains of Western Europe.

Retrace steps back along the crest of the Great Blasket, crossing Croaghmore and Slievedonagh. On the descent towards the next prominent saddle, remember that there is a junction of paths at the 'Traffic Lights'. At this stage, you can take the path to the right for an alternative return to the village. The path is mostly pleasant and grassy, contouring across a steep slope. When a pronounced left bend is reached, the ruins and few remaining houses of the village suddenly come into view. Simply zigzag down the grassy tracks back into the village. Any spare time before the ferry leaves can be used exploring the ruins or simply visiting the craft shop and cafe.

Blasket Island Literature
Copies of the various books written by Blasket Islanders can be obtained at the Great Blasket Visitor Centre at Dunquin. While on the island, there may be guided tours of the ruined village, pointing out the homes of some of the islanders, with particular reference to those places once inhabited by the writers. There is a map available locally which records the islanders' names for practically every little cove and rocky buttress around the island.

WALK 18
The Three Sisters

Looking for all the world like a tidal wave of rock set four-square against the breakers of the Atlantic Ocean, Sybil Head and the Three Sisters form a remarkable rocky ridge. This fine coastal walk can be approached from Ballyferriter and can be conveniently started from the Dún an Óir Golf Hotel. A narrow path can be traced almost all the way along the crest, rather like a roller-coaster route, with superb coastal and mountain views in clear weather. A low-level stretch of the Dingle Way allows a circular route to be followed.

The Route

Distance:	8 miles (13 kilometres).
Start:	Dún an Óir Golf Hotel, Ballyferriter - 329056.
Map:	OS Discovery Sheet 70.
Terrain:	Narrow cliff paths with plenty of ups and downs, as well as tracks and roads on lower ground.
Parking:	Ask permission at the Dún an Óir Golf Hotel.
Transport:	Bus Eireann table numbers 276 & 281 serve nearby Ballyferriter.

The Dún an Óir Golf Hotel is a rather startling collection of white buildings providing accommodation, food and drink, as well as parking for patrons. Other motorists should ask permission to park. Bus services can sometimes be rather sparse through nearby Ballyferriter. Leave the hotel by walking up the road alongside. A Dingle Way marker points right, but turn left to follow a road and track past some farm buildings. After passing the highest building a junction of tracks is reached. Turn left and walk to the end of the track, then turn right and follow a narrow path uphill. This starts on short grass, then as the ground steepens the grass becomes longer

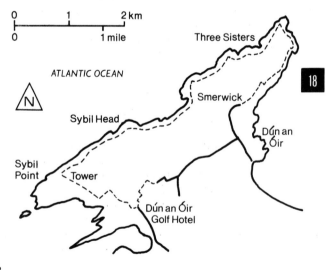

and the ground can be wet. Aim for a ruined tower on top of Sybil Point at 676ft (206m). The crest of the ridge is fairly sharp and the cliffs fall precipitously to the sea. Looking along the crest, the Three Sisters stand in line, with Brandon Mountain rising beyond. In the other direction, the Blasket Islands can be seen. In certain lights the effect is stunning.

Follow a narrow path beside a fence, wherever possible on the seaward side, rather than in the small fields on the gentler landward slope. The crest of the ridge is made of a coarse conglomerate rock often covered in heather or bracken. As progress is made, views back to the ruined tower are amazing, as it appears to be perched on top of a pyramidal peak of rock. The way ahead is like a switchback, but generally downhill, though there is a little peak to climb at Sybil Head before a more pronounced gap is reached. Enjoy the views of rugged cliff scenery before following an embankment across a wide, low gap.

The slope up to the first of the Three Sisters is rugged and heathery, but there is a narrow path. Cross over the summit and descend to a gap. The second peak is slightly easier to climb, and a short, steep slope of grass leads down the far side. There is a rugged crest to follow before the true gap is reached further along. The last of the Three Sisters appears to be a fine pyramidal peak, with heather slopes giving way to a blade-like summit of rock. Few walkers would care to stand on such a precipitous perch! Enjoy the views for one last time before descending. A narrow coastal path runs alongside Smerwick Harbour, linking with a track at a gate, which leads to a series of farms and houses at Smerwick.

A road runs through Smerwick and bends left. Turn right at a road junction and walk straight on, noting the exotic vegetation alongside the road. There are also old glasshouses, which are all that remain of a former tomato-growing industry. Keep to the right at a road junction and follow the road into a farmyard. A track leads onwards, but turn left as indicated by a Dingle Way marker post to reach the Sybil Head Golf Course. Walk around the top edge of the golf course until another marker post shows an exit onto a grassy track near the clubhouse. Follow the track and turn right along the golf course access road. A left turn leads back to the Dún an Óir Golf Hotel.

Dún an Óir

The 'Golden Fort' of Dún an Óir is nowhere near the Dún an Óir Golf Hotel, but is actually off-route near Smerwick. The promontory on which the ancient fort is located overlooks Smerwick Harbour. It was here that a force of 600 Spanish and Irish soldiers surrendered to an English force in 1580. Despite being offered a safe passage, they were slaughtered on the spot, with the countryside round about being devastated afterwards.

WALK 19

The Magharees

One stretch of the Dingle Way runs around the Magharees Peninsula and is essentially a low-level walk. The Magharees, or Seven Hogs, are a group of rugged little islands, two of which are joined to the mainland by a belt of sand dunes. The walk around the Magharees can be accomplished from Castlegregory, taking in a couple of old church sites and sweeping sandy beaches. The belts of sand dunes on either side of the peninsula enclose Lough Gill and the area is a notable haunt of natterjack toads.

The Route

Distance:	13½ miles (22 kilometres).
Start:	Castlegregory - 621133.
Maps:	OS Discovery Sheets 70 & 71.
Terrain:	Easy walking along roads, beaches and grassy coastal paths. Very high tides could make the beach walks impassable.
Parking:	Plenty of spaces around Castlegregory.
Transport:	Bus Eireann table number 273 offers a limited service to Castlegregory.

Castlegregory is a colourful, tidy, interesting little place, with abundant shops and pubs, as well as accommodation. Follow Main Street and turn left along West Main Street to leave, following signs for Cloghane and Brandon. After passing the last couple of pubs, the road runs through fields with occasional glimpses of Lough Gill to

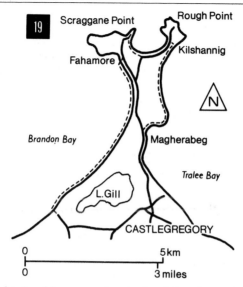

19 Scraggane Point   Rough Point

Fahamore   Kilshannig

Brandon Bay   Magherabeg

Tralee Bay

L.Gill

CASTLEGREGORY

```
0              5km
├──────────────┤
0              3 miles
```

the right. An old graveyard and ruined church stand alongside the
Church of Ireland at Killiney. Turn right along a narrow road
signposted for Stradbally Strand, passing more fields, then turn
right to cross a bridge and pass another ruined church at the old
Stradbally graveyard. The road passes an area of reeds before
reaching a gap in the sand dunes giving access to the broad sweep
of Brandon Bay.

Turn right to walk along the strand, which is mostly firm sand,
with dunes covered in marram grass rising above. A very high tide
could press walkers against the dune belt and make the way
forward impassable for a while. When the tide is out, there is plenty
of space to wander, and range upon range of mountains rise further
inland. The cluster of buildings at Fahamore can be seen in the
distance and all walkers need to do is walk towards them. Later, the
beach becomes quite bouldery and a Dingle Way marker post at a
gap in the dunes shows the way onto a minor road. Turn left to
follow the road away from the sea, passing Spillane's Bar on the way
through Fahamore. When the road reaches the sea again, there are
views of some of the islands off the end of the point. A right turn

A Dingle Way marker post beside Brandon Bay

leads past Harbour House B&B and Waterworld overlooking Scraggane Bay.

The road runs to a pier and small harbour at Scraggane Bay, but don't follow it. Instead, turn right along a narrow coastal path, through little fields of grass and vegetables. The path is on a crumbling edge of boulder clay, and may need care in places. The path joins another minor road to continue around Scraggane Bay, but it is also possible to walk along a grassy embankment above the road. Kilshannig is the next little settlement, and there is a ruined church worth visiting.

Leave Kilshannig by cutting straight towards Tralee Bay along a track. The Dingle Way is routed along the beach, but this can be uncomfortably stony and walkers may prefer staying ashore. There is a grassy edge, sometimes with a narrow trodden path, outside of any fencing which occurs later. A prominent sandy track reaches the shore, then the reedy pool of Lough Naparka is reached. A more rugged stretch of dunes is threaded by vague paths, while anyone walking along the shore will be walking on rock. Either way, a short walk leads around Magherabeg Beach to a small caravan site, car park and toilets. An information board lists a range of birds which might be spotted.

Turn left to walk along a coastal road buttressed by boulders. The road drifts inland to cross the Trench Bridge, where water flows from Lough Gill to the sea. The road continues inland passing fields to return to Castlegregory. Turn left at Post Office Square to return to Main Street in the centre of town. There are plenty of places offering food and drink.

The Magharees
The sand dunes and pools of the Magharees are notable for their large population of natterjack toads. The breeding season is from mid-April to mid-June, accompanied by raucous croaking. Tadpoles need to mature into toadlets before their pools dry out. Mortality rates can be high at this time, but the toads have a poisonous secretion which keeps most predators at bay. By mid-autumn the toads begin to hibernate in burrows until the following spring.

Kilshannig Church
The ruined church in the graveyard at Kilshannig is associated with St. Senach. An unusual feature is a stone slab inscribed with a Chi-Rho cross ending in a series of spirals. This may pre-date the ruins, which are mainly 15th to 16th century, with traces of an earlier structure.

WALK 20
Kerry Head

Kerry Head is a rugged peninsula with some interesting features, but it is also tough to traverse on foot and some of the paths are along very narrow, exposed lines above the cliffs. There are two fine promontory forts on the westernmost parts of the headland, while the roads and tracks further inland have been waymarked as part of the North Kerry Way. Walkers are again reminded that the first parts of the route are quite exposed in places and require a measure of agility and a head for heights.

The Route

Distance:	6 miles (10 kilometres).
Start:	Tiduff, Kerry Head - 698301.
Maps:	OS Discovery Sheets 63 & 71.
Terrain:	Some very narrow and exposed cliff walking, becoming easier later, ending with a track and road.
Parking:	Very limited at a road junction at Tiduff.
Transport:	Bus Eireann table number 274 serves nearby Ballyheigue.

Parking for cars is very restricted at the start of this walk and the nearest point reached by bus is Ballyheigue. Motorists can follow Kerry Head Ring signposts from Ballyheigue, uphill through Glenderry to a signposted road junction where there is a small shelter. There might be room to park a car around this junction. Start the walk by heading back down the road, passing a few houses, turning right at an unsignposted road junction. The road leads to a huddle of houses and farms where a left turn is made. (A right turn, incidentally, leads to an interesting old graveyard at Cill Mhic a' Deaghadh.) Walk through the farmyard and straight down a couple of fields to reach the cliffs.

Take a look to the right along the cliff-line and consider if this is your type of walk. A very vague and narrow path leads along a

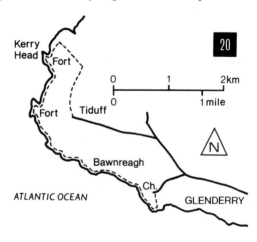

narrow, uneven strip between an embankment and the cliff edge. This is used by a few fishermen heading for the rock platforms further along. Walkers will need to make progress along this narrow strip, and other similar strips, sometimes walking through fields just inland. There are abundant growths of thrift, among other flowers, and the cliff scenery is impressive in places. When a little valley needs to be crossed, look carefully for the circular ramparts of an ancient rath. There are some brambly and stony patches further along, but nothing which should bar progress.

The field boundaries come to an end and the westernmost parts of Kerry Head are sloping moorlands. Look out for two rocky points where parallel embankments are all that remain of two ancient promontory forts. These are worth investigating, and the cliffs between them feature a fine rock arch. Views stretch from the mountainous Dingle Peninsula to the more regular lines of Loop Head. Continue onwards across a rugged slope of grass and heather which is squelchy in places. There are also stony patches and areas of ground-hugging gorse. Look carefully for signs of a low, overgrown embankment which leads straight uphill; it isn't too easy to spot, so refer to the map. The embankment is an ancient earthwork called An Clia Rua. It can be followed uphill to reach an obvious moorland track.

Turn right to follow the track, which is part of the North Kerry Way. It leads to some large farm buildings and can be rather muddy at that point. A waymark post points to the left along a tarmac road. Follow the road past several houses and small farms, all looking towards the cliffs and the mountains of the Dingle peninsula. The end of the walk is reached at the first road junction, beside the small shelter.

Cill Mhic a' Deaghadh

The old graveyard which can be visited just before the cliff walk contains a ruined church dedicated to St. Erc, son of Deaghadh. Erc was a bishop who lived at Leirg and was associated with St. Brendan the Voyager. He died in AD 512 and was buried on Dunmore Head overlooking the Blasket Islands. The old graveyard is unusual in that it is reserved exclusively for the burial of local Corridan family members.

WALK 21

Loop Head

It's a determined walker who beats a path to Loop Head; a battered peninsula between the Mouth of the Shannon and the Atlantic Ocean. Kilkee is the nearest seaside resort, while Kilbaha is the last village, after which there is only a straggle of farms and a lighthouse. There is a trodden path, very vague in places, around the cliffs from Kilbaha. If time is pressing, then at least cover the very end of the headland near the lighthouse. Despite the apparent isolation, Loop Head shows signs of ancient habitations. Views of Kerry Head and Brandon Mountain give way to more distant views of the Aran Islands and Connemara in clear weather.

The Route

Distance:	9¹/₂ miles (15 kilometres).
Start:	Kilbaha - 738482.
Map:	OS Discovery Sheet 63.
Terrain:	Cliff paths can be vague and uneven at first, ending with a short road walk.
Parking:	At the Lighthouse Inn, Kilbaha.
Transport:	Bus Eireann table number 336 offers a Tuesday service to Kilbaha. Table numbers 15 & 50 offer more regular services to nearby Kilkee.

While there are buses to Kilkee every day of the week, Kilbaha is served by bus only on Tuesdays, but there are a couple of B&Bs which might collect you by arrangement. Cars simply follow the R487 road to Kilbaha, or follow the signposted Loop Drive, and park near the Lighthouse Inn.

Walk away from the Lighthouse Inn and keep left at the New Inn to reach a small quay. Look for a small quayside memorial to Fr. Meehan, who used to say Mass from a hut on wheels known as the Little Ark; more about this towards the end of the walk. A grassy path leaves the quay and runs through small fields. Be prepared to step across low fences, some of which are electrified, and there are some low embankments also to be crossed. A certain amount of

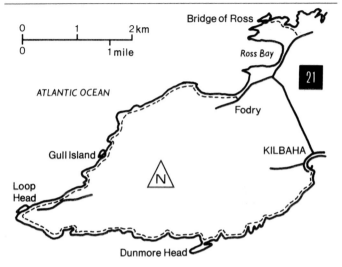

agility is needed at first, but there are no real obstacles. A small lookout tower is passed and there is a more substantial ruin further inland. Look carefully for the path, as it is vague in places and eventually you should switch to the rough strip of ground between the fields and the cliffs.

Some practical advice; whenever you notice the field boundaries moving further inland, be ready to find narrow, rock-walled chasms full of boulders and the surging sea. A farm is just uphill, close to where a series of these chasms is passed. The next feature of interest is Dunmore Head, which is the site of a promontory fort. The sea has breached a rock wall to form the headland, and note how the sea has scoured out the loose glacial drift to leave a natural embankment which would have been the only approach to the fort. There is a tunnel through Dunmore Head which is full of sea water.

There are rock platforms as well as cliffs and chasms along the coast, while a rock-walled bay contains a fine sea stack. The westernmost part of the headland features open slopes above cliffs which gradually rise higher and higher and there are cushions of thrift growing. As the point of Loop Head is turned, a narrow, deep chasm full of the surging sea separates Dermot and Grania's Rock from the mainland. There is a cairn only a short distance away, but inaccessible to visitors. Continue past the whitewashed walls enclosing the lighthouse buildings, and keep to the cliff path, rather than the nearby lighthouse access road. As the next headland is reached, the separation between Dermot and Grania's Rock and the mainland is easier to appreciate.

A fine grassy cliff path stays well away from the fields and there is a view of a pierced headland. Chaotic scenery surrounds Gull Island, then a broad heath stretches back from the cliffs. When fences and embankments encroach towards the cliffs again, a narrow, grassy strip can be followed. This strip is crumbling, so at times you may have to use the cobbly beach instead. Eventually, a narrow road is reached and this is followed by turning left. At the next junction, either turn right to complete the walk, or turn left to walk to the Bridge of Ross, where a rock arch covered in short green grass presents an unusual spectacle. When the road cutting back across the headland to Kilbaha is followed, note that the Roman Catholic church along the way contains an unusual structure known as the Little Ark.

Dermot and Grania's Rock
The wall of rock which is completely severed from Loop Head is known as Dermot and Grania's Rock. Grania was supposed to marry the warrior Fionn Mac Cumhail, but ran away with Dermot instead. As they were pursued all over Ireland by Fionn, one of the places the runaways reached was Loop Head. The name is derived from 'Leap Head', as the lovers leapt across the chasm in a dramatic escape bid.

The Little Ark
This is housed in the Roman Catholic church at Kilbaha and is basically a hut on wheels. It was used as a mobile church from 1852, allowing Fr. Meehan to travel around the area and say Mass down on the shore, where the harsh penal laws forbidding such religious services could not be enforced. A memorial beside the harbour at Kilbaha marks one of the sites which was used by Fr. Meehan and his Little Ark.

WALK 22

Cliffs of Moher

The walk along the Cliffs of Moher is one of the most popular coastal walks in Ireland. A visitor centre and large car park are a mere stroll from a precipitous cliff, so hordes of people can be expected in the summer months. There are far fewer visitors at other times, but it is rare to have the place entirely to yourself. O'Brien's Tower stands above the most popular part of the cliff, while the ruins of Moher Tower are seen to the south-west. People are accustomed to walk along the cliff-line between the two towers, though in recent years the right to do so has been challenged. The situation may be resolved, or you may be able to proceed no further than the popular part of the cliffs. Either way, the view is for free!

The Route

Distance:	6 miles (10 kilometres).
Start:	Cliffs of Moher Visitor Centre - 042922.
Maps:	OS Discovery Sheets 51 & 57.
Terrain:	Well-worn paths along a sheer cliff edge.
Parking:	At the Cliffs of Moher Visitor Centre.
Transport:	Bus Eireann table numbers 50 & 337 serve nearby Doolin.

The Cliffs of Moher Visitor Centre sells all manner of souvenirs and has a restaurant and toilets, but most people will be eager to reach the cliffs. It all happens rather suddenly; there they are in all their glory. A wall

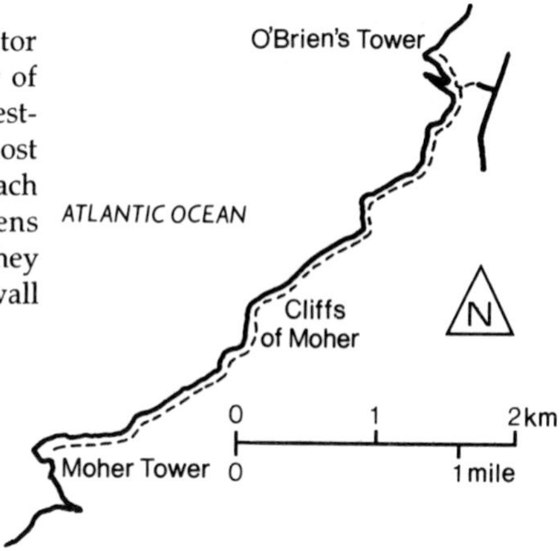

O'Brien's Tower

ATLANTIC OCEAN

Cliffs of Moher

N

Moher Tower

0   1   2 km

0   1 mile

22

is flanked with warning notices, but people simply skip over it and lie on their bellies looking straight down at the crashing waves of the Atlantic Ocean. To the right is O'Brien's Tower, which is reached by climbing steps. The view along the cliffs to the distant Moher Tower on Hag's Head is superb.

Route directions are scarcely needed. A deeply worn path can be seen climbing uphill beyond the point where visitors swarm around the cliff edge. Following this path, you always have the sheer cliffs to your right, and an assortment of fences, turf banks and stone walls to your left. There are some stiles to cross, while other stiles may be blocked. Either way, the path along the cliffs is clear throughout. There is a small quarry to pass, where slabs of rock have been lifted from the ground, leaving a notch in the cliff-line. Beware of electric fences along this stretch, as a sudden shock so near to the cliff edge could have unfortunate consequences.

The path twists and turns as it runs parallel to the cliff edge, but it also rises and falls. The result is that views are constantly changing along the way, and there may be a variety of birds to spot soaring on the updraught or nesting on ledges. The blocky outline of Moher Tower eventually dominates the scene and there are fine views back to O'Brien's Tower, as well as closer to hand around Hag's Head. The Aran Islands can be seen out to sea in clear weather, but from this angle all three can appear merged into one. In very clear weather the mountains of Connemara can appear in a rugged line beyond the islands.

To return to the visitor centre, simply retrace steps along the cliff top and enjoy the experience all over again.

Burren Way

When the Burren Way was first waymarked over the hills and along the coast, it included this particular stretch of the Cliffs of Moher. It was routed inside the fields, however, rather than along the edge of the cliffs, and some of the stiles can be seen in the adjacent fields. This was a strange way to take the route, as practically every visitor walks along the cliff edge. Furthermore, the moment that access difficulties first became apparent, the route was summarily closed and taken along a tarmac road well away from the sea. Again, a strange move, as walkers still favour following the cliffs.

WALK 23

Inis Oírr

Inis Oírr is the smallest of the three Aran Islands and although it is usually very quiet it can be busy in the summer. A walk around the coast of the island is relatively easy to accomplish, but some parts can be rough and bouldery. The circuit may be completed between ferries, but this may result in rushing around at certain times, and it is of course necessary to have up-to-date timetables to hand. There are hostel and B&B accommodation options, as well as shops and pubs.

The Route

Distance:	6 miles (10 kilometres).
Start:	At the pier at An Baile Thíos - 979030.
Maps:	OS Discovery Sheet 51. OS Aran Islands Map.
Terrain:	Roads, tracks and paths, but also some bouldery and rocky areas.
Parking:	Cars cannot be taken to the island. There are car parks on the mainland.
Transport:	Ferries run round the year from Rosaveal, and in the summer from Galway and Doolin. Aer Árann operate flights around the year from Inverin.

Start on the pier at An Baile Thíos and turn left. The road later turns inland to reach a mound called Cnoc Raithní, then turns left to run between a sports pitch and a beach amenity area. The road rises between a school and a hilltop graveyard, where an ancient church has been excavated. The Aer Árann airstrip is passed, then the road runs within sight of Lough More, which is hemmed in between low cliffs. When the tarmac ends in a series of small fields, a gravel track continues.

A prominent feature to the left is the rusting wreck of the ship Plassey, with the Burren and Cliffs of Moher seen beyond. Note the stone platforms beside the track, which have been constructed for the drying of seaweed. When a tarmac road appears and heads inland, keep instead to the bouldery shore, following a very rough

85

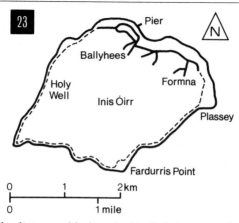

track. In the distance a black and white lighthouse can be seen and the route runs towards it. The final approach uses a road flanked by stout, straight walls. There is no admittance to the lighthouse compound, so cross a stone stile to pass the final walled enclosure.

Keep seawards of dozens of tiny, walled fields, picking a way across bouldery terrain. A couple of road-ends are passed where the walking is easier. Later, there is a bouldery point to be turned and it may be better to walk a bit further inland on an open limestone pavement. After passing the end of a grassy track, a gravelly coastal track develops, with boulders to the left and fields to the right. Although at times the terrain can look like a limestone desert, there is in fact a profuse plant-life. As the first few houses are approached, there is plenty of bare limestone to the left of the road. Keep left at a junction of narrow roads to be led back to the pier. There is immediate access to food and drink, as well as accommodation.

Inis Oírr Way

The yellow marker arrows of the Inis Oírr Way are encountered at the beginning and end of the coastal walk. The waymarked route stays mainly around the inhabited part of the island, describing loops on roads and tracks to include a number of important features. Most notable is Dún Fhormna, where an ancient stone cashel on a hilltop has a later castle rising from its centre. The castle belonged to the O'Briens, who owned the island up to 1585. A prominent signal tower nearby was built in 1804. The route also visits the small monastic site of Cill na Seacht nInion, the holy well of Tobar Éinne and the ruined church called Cill Ghobnait. Other features on the route are seen on the coastal circuit. The Inis Oírr Way measures 6 miles (10 kilometres).

Cnoc Raithní

In 1885 gales exposed a curious mound and drystone walling, containing pottery urns, cremated human bones and a small bronze pin. The mound was a Bronze Age structure dating from 1500BC, but nearby were two dozen stone-lined graves from the Early Christian Period, indicating a continual use of the site for burials.

Teampall Chaomháin

Excavated from a sandy mound used as a graveyard, Teampall Chaomháin is a remarkable church. St. Caomhán was the brother of St. Kevin of Glendalough, and the ground plan of the church is similar to that of Trinity Church in distant Glendalough. The church may date from the 10th century but has been widened and restructured. The heavy lintelled doorway is from the original church, but the sacristy is medieval. In a separate small building is the grave of St. Caomhán which, like the church, has been excavated from tons of windblown sand.

WALK 24

Inis Meáin

Inis Meáin is the middle of the three Aran Islands, and possibly the quietest at most times of the year. A walk around its coast can be achieved by linking roads, tracks and paths, but there is also some rugged walking on rock and heaps of boulders. The cliffs of Creaga Dubha are quite dramatic, but are seldom seen by visitors. The circuit described can be completed in a few hours, but might not always be possible between ferries. Accommodation is quite limited, though there are a couple of shops and a pub on the island.

The Route

Distance:	9 miles (14 kilometres).
Start:	At the pier at An Córa - 946046.
Maps:	OS Discovery Sheet 51. OS Aran Islands Map.
Terrain:	Roads, tracks and paths for half the circuit, but also rocky and bouldery ground and a sandy beach walk.
Parking:	Cars cannot be taken to the island. There are car parks on the mainland.
Transport:	Ferries run round the year from Rosaveal, and in the summer from Galway and Doolin. Aer Árann operate flights around the year from Inverin.

Starting from the pier at An Córa, turn left as signposted for Cill Cheannanach, following a stony and grassy track beside heaps of boulders. The track turns inland to pass close to the tiny ruined church of St. Cheannanach, which is surrounded by grave slabs. The track twists and turns uphill, climbing from terrace to terrace to reach a tarmac road near a house. Views across Foul Sound embrace the Burren, Inis Oírr and the Cliffs of Moher. Turn left to follow the road past a house and continue beyond the end of the tarmac. A grassy and stony track continues onwards, passing several walled

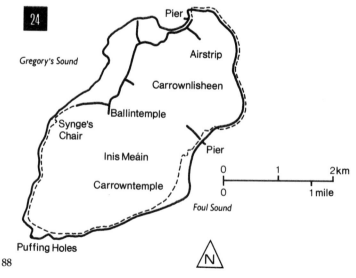

fields and inclining gently towards the sea.

A little thatched hut is reached on the top of a low cliff. Keep following the track, later passing the end of a grassy track. Continue along a narrow path which has been cleared through heaps of boulders. Later, the cliff-line is so low that it is easier to walk along a rocky platform instead of walking on boulders. Don't stray too far seawards, as the rocks can be rather wet and slippery. Another grassy track might be noticed leading down through the fields. A tall memorial cairn is also a good marker.

Keep to the rock platform as the boulders are quite extensive around the southern end of the island. Depending on the state of the tide and the weather, look out for the Puffing Holes, where the sea is occasionally forced to spout skywards from the rock. Again, don't go too close to the sea as the rock can be slippery. After turning round the southern end of the island, rock terraces and ramps gradually lead higher and higher, and the cliffs of Creaga Dubha are quite dramatic. Take care near the edge, as they are also deeply undercut. Looking across Gregory's Sound, Kilronan and Inis Mór can be seen, while further away are the Twelve Bens and Maum Turk Mountains. A prominent cairn is reached on a bouldery area high above the sea, then more cairns are passed; one of which is a windbreak known as Synge's Chair, used as a viewpoint by John Millington Synge.

Walk down a short, steep, rocky slope and bear right to follow the cliff edge. Cross a stile over the first wall encountered, then keep to the cliff edge to reach the end of a road. Follow the road, which drifts inland away from a very rough and bouldery stretch of coast. After passing a couple of houses, turn left and follow another road onto the lower, northern part of the island. At the next road junction, turn left again to follow a road across bare limestone, between fields and down through a rock cutting to cross a bouldery storm beach.

The track heads inland with a grassy surface. Continue through gates and pass a stone hut, then later go through a gate on the left which leads onto a broad and rocky area. Turn right to walk beside a wall, then go through a small gate on the right. Turn immediately left to follow a path downhill and through a gap in a wall. After gaining the coast again, turn right to walk along a cobbly storm beach, away from a stone shelter. Eventually, a narrow road is reached and this can be followed to a stout concrete pier.

Keep to the shore, following a narrow, grassy strip beside stone walls. Later, the ground becomes quite bouldery, but it is possible to drop down to a broad, sandy beach. This is backed by dunes, beyond which is the Aer Árann airstrip. When the sandy beach gives way to more boulders, come ashore and either pick up vague paths, or walk along the top of a low line of cliffs. Eventually, the small, sandy beach of Trá Leitreach is reached, and there is a narrow tarmac road beside a graveyard. Follow the road, and although it later turns inland, it turns left to run straight back to the pier at An Córa where the walk started.

Inis Meáin Way

The yellow marker arrows of the Inis Meáin Way are encountered in a few places on the coastal walk. The waymarked route stays mainly around the inhabited part of the island, describing loops on roads and tracks to include a number of important features. Most notable are Dún Fhearbhaí and Dún Chonchúir, where ancient stone cashels crown hilltop sites. A couple of ruined church sites, and a house used by John Millington Synge are passed, and the route also includes some features of modern island life and work. The Inis Meáin Way measures 5 miles (8 kilometres).

St. Ceannanach

Several theories are advanced for the name of this ancient church, which may have become confused with the passage of time. The structure is quite small, being an oratory or very simple church, dating prior to 1200. A heavy lintelled doorway and large stones are features of its construction. Projecting corbel stones from the gables are similar to early churches at Glendalough, and were used for supporting roof timbers.

WALK 25

Inis Mór

Inis Mór is the largest and busiest of the three Aran Islands. Regular ferry services dock at Kilronan and there are flights to a nearby airstrip. The island has a good range of shops, pubs, restaurants and accommodation options. Minibuses meet the ferries and take visitors to wherever they want on the island. The southern coastline is entirely rocky and the cliffs are often sheer or even undercut by the sea. A walk along the length of this coast is recommended. The waymarked Inis Mór Way allows the northern coast and island interior to be explored.

The Route

Distance:	15 miles (24 kilometres).
Start:	At the slipway near the Brannock Islands - 777116.
Finish:	Kilronan - 883088.
Map:	OS Discovery Sheet 51. OS Aran Islands Map.
Terrain:	Mostly rocky and often bouldery, ending with paths, tracks and roads.
Parking:	Cars cannot be taken to the island. There are car parks on the mainland.
Transport:	Ferries run around the year from Rosaveal, and in the summer from Galway and Doolin. Aer Árann operate flights around the year from Inverin. There are several minibuses operating services on the island.

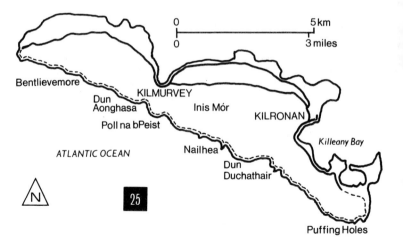

Take a minibus ride to the western end of Inis Mór, where the road ends at a small slipway facing the lighthouse on the Brannock Islands, with a view of the Twelve Bens on the mainland. There is a hut before the slipway, and the walk starts by crossing the wall on the opposite side of the road. After a short walk a rocky point is reached where a little height is gained, then suddenly there is a view all the way along the southern cliffs of Inis Mór, and even to the tapering end of Inis Meáin, with the Cliffs of Moher beyond. Take note of the rugged ground in view ahead, and of the limestone pavements, and the overhanging cliff edges. The whole day's walk is across this sort of terrain.

After crossing a bouldery gap, walls need to be crossed over and over again as the ground rises towards the higher cliffs. Most walls run to the very edge of the cliff, but they may be low enough to step over easily. Others may be equipped with stone step stiles or gap stiles, and it is worth looking for these rather than climbing and risking damaging walls. Some walls run parallel to the cliff edges, leaving only a narrow strip to walk along, where it is important to remember that the edge may be overhanging. Spring gentians are a feature of some high stretches, but there are many other flowers throughout the year.

The cliff-line leads to the semi-circular fort of Dún Aonghasa, which should be explored thoroughly. Continue by walking down a rugged slope, turning round a deeply undercut semi-circular cliff at An Sunda Caoch. After turning a bare, rocky point at the far side, note the rectangular trough of Poll na bPéist, which the sea feeds from above and below. Walk along rock platforms above the sea, avoiding huge boulders for a while. Later, the cliffs increase in height and the walking is on coarse, broken limestone. Cross walls as required, noting erratic boulders of granite on the pavements further inland. Again, there are walls running parallel to the cliff edge. The long promontory at Nailhea is flanked by some dramatically rocky bays, then height is gradually lost, though the cliffs themselves remain as rugged as ever.

The promontory fort of Dún Dúchathair is on an undercut headland, and again the fort should be explored thoroughly. There is no doorway, so go round the far end of the wall to see the internal structures. Continue around the next undercut semi-circular cliff-

Poll na bPéist is a natural rectangular hole on Inis Mór

line, walking across some very rocky ground. It is best to walk along rock platforms above the sea, rather than on the huge boulders alongside. Further inland, stone walls bound numerous fields and there is no really easy surface to walk along. Further along, however, when the rock platform becomes too narrow for comfort, cross the boulders and follow the field walls for a while. A broad gravel track will be encountered and this can be followed, though it suddenly expires in another rocky area. At that point, switch to the rock platforms above the sea again.

As the southern end of Inis Mór is being turned, look out for the Puffing Holes. These have been formed where deep caves excavated by the sea have collapsed at some point inland, so that when the sea is in a furious mood spray may be periodically ejected from the hole in the limestone pavement. Beyond this point, stay close to the cliff edge, passing below an old tower stump, to pick up a path leading through some small fields. At length, turn left to follow another path straight to a road-end further inland.

The narrow road leads past a few houses at Iaráirne, then passes a graveyard where the ruined church of Teaghlach Éinne can be inspected. Next, the road passes the Aer Árann airstrip near the broad, sandy bay of An Trá Mhór, running through the village of Cill Éinne afterwards. There is a pub and restaurant, as well as accommodation, a ruined castle and a small pier. The road continues a little inland for a while, passing some Leachta Cuimhne, or memorial stones. The final part of the road runs around a bay to reach the village of Kilronan, where this walk ends.

Dún Aonghasa
This semi-circular cliff-top fort stands on top of a 245ft (75m) overhanging cliff. The central area is surrounded by a terraced rampart, further surrounded by two more stone ramparts and a formidable band of razor-sharp 'chevaux de frise'. It may have been built in stages from 800BC and been spasmodically occupied until around AD800. Its structure has been altered considerably through the ages and the stout supporting buttresses were constructed during 19th century restoration.

Dún Dúchathair
This fort occupies a cliff-bound promontory and consists of a terraced rampart surrounded by a band of 'chevaux de frise'. There are a series of walled hut sites clustered alongside the rampart, as well as traces of other hut sites in a bouldery area near the cliff edge.

Cill Éinne
Almost buried in a sandy graveyard, the ruins of Teaghlach Éinne can be inspected. Another church site near Cill Éinne is Teampall Bheanáin, and the base of a round tower and cross can be seen nearby. These are all that remain of a monastic enclosure. The tiny harbour is dominated by the ruins of Caisleán Aircín.

Kilronan
The only real large settlement on Inis Mór is the village of Kilronan. Here are concentrated most of the shops, pubs, restaurants and accommodation options. Ferries reach Kilronan from Rosaveal, Galway and Doolin, as well as from Inis Meáin and Inis Oírr. Most ferries are met by an assortment of minibuses which take people to all parts of the island.

unfenced expanse of short grass can offer walks in any direction on dry land, even to the low, cairned summit of the island where fine views can be enjoyed. Either way, continue walking around the island to reach a prominent bay. A small Holy Well can be studied near the head of the bay. Head slightly inland to reach a large expanse of water called Lough Fahy. A track on the grass leads off to the right towards some houses. Turn left to reach and follow a tarmac road through the middle of the island. This road runs onto Omey Strand and marker posts across the sands lead back to the mainland near Claddaghduff Quay.

WALK 27

Killary Harbour

One of the best short coastal walks in Connemara is along the southern shore of Killary Harbour, following a fine old road from Bunowen to Killary Harbour Youth Hostel. The route is linear and Bunowen can occasionally be reached by bus services, while a handy youth hostel is located at the end of the walk. The huge mountain of Mweelrea dominates the narrow fjord-like sea inlet from start to finish. Rafts and barrels mark the location of salmon cages and mussel beds which have been sited along the sheltered inlet.

The Route

Distance:	5 miles (8 kilometres).
Start:	On the main road at Bunowen - 822607.
Finish:	Killary Harbour Youth Hostel - 769649.
Map:	OS Discovery Sheet 37.
Terrain:	A road and good tracks, but some parts can be wet.
Parking:	Limited roadside space at Bunowen and a small space on the quay at Killary Harbour.
Transport:	Bus Eireann table numbers 419, 420 & 61 offer a limited and seasonal service to Bunowen, but there is no service from the youth hostel.

Start on the main N59 road at Bunowen, where a narrow, unenclosed

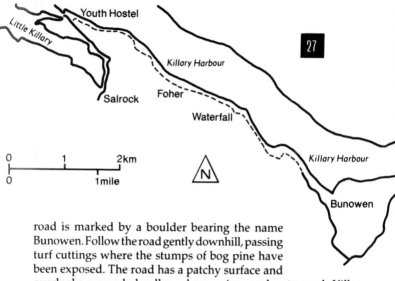

road is marked by a boulder bearing the name Bunowen. Follow the road gently downhill, passing turf cuttings where the stumps of bog pine have been exposed. The road has a patchy surface and overlooks a wooded valley where a river rushes to reach Killary Harbour. The mountain of Mweelrea rises beyond. After passing a couple of houses and farm buildings, go through a gate on a gentle rise on the road.

Tarmac gives way to a broad gravel track, running gently down a rugged moorland slope. A small stand of conifers are passed and there is a house just beyond the trees. A boathouse and slipway are located beside the sea, and are associated with the fishery industry on Killary Harbour. Cross a stile beside a gate and continue along the track. The way is unenclosed, with a few trees growing alongside. Cross another stile beside another gate, then cross a concrete bridge where a waterfall tumbles down to the sea. The track becomes more grassy and can be wet and muddy in places, with a low stone wall on the seaward side. A small cottage is passed at Foher, with another cottage nearby and the ruins of other buildings scattered around some old fields.

Keep following the grassy track, passing through a small gate in a wall, then climbing a stile over the next wall. There is a short, steep stretch where the track has been cut into a rocky cliff, then the rest of the line is unfenced, but shows distinct signs of engineering. The surrounding slopes are boggy and rocky, but the track is clear and obvious to follow. Some parts may be quite narrow and stony, or even cross bare rock. A drystone wall diverts the track away from the sea and leads it towards a cottage and a minor road. Turn right along the road to reach the quayside next to Killary Harbour Youth Hostel.

Killary Harbour

This long sea inlet is a true glacial fjord, being long and narrow and bounded by mountains. It is deeper along its length than at its mouth, which is almost blocked by the island of Inis Bearna. In 1903 a British naval fleet weighed anchor to allow King Edward VII and Queen Alexandra to make a sightseeing tour of Connemara.

Killary Harbour Youth Hostel

This was formerly Rosroe Cottage and a plaque fixed to the wall records: 'Ludwig Wittgenstein, 1889-1951, Philosopher, lived and worked here April 1948 - Oct 1948.' The quayside nearby usually features an assortment of lobster pots and small boats, while the Killary Salmon Fishery can be seen a short distance away.

WALK 28

Inishbofin

Although it looks small in size, Inishbofin has an amazingly indented coastline, so that tracing its perimeter is a hefty day's walk. A succession of rugged headlands and bays ensure constant variety and interest. There are small, rocky islets offshore, including Inishark and its deserted village. On the approach to Inishbofin, note the length of the harbour, and study the star-shaped Cromwell's Fort which guards it. Initial views of the land around the village lead visitors to believe that this is a fertile island, but in fact much of it is bleak and barren.

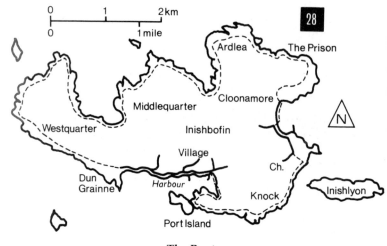

The Route

Distance:	14 miles (23 kilometres).
Start:	At the pier in Bofin Harbour - 536648.
Map:	OS Discovery Sheet 37.
Terrain:	Some roads and tracks, but mostly pathless slopes and rugged cliff walking.
Parking:	Cars cannot be taken to the island. Parking available at Cleggan.
Transport:	Bus Eireann table number 419 serves Cleggan. Ferries serve Inishbofin from Cleggan.

Leave the pier and turn right to follow the road around Bofin Harbour, passing the church to reach Day's Hotel. Either follow the shore at low tide, or turn left and right to pass above the hotel. Another right turn down a grassy track leads to the shore, where a scanty series of paths can be used to cross low rock headlands. Go through three gates around the head of the harbour, aiming towards Cromwell's Fort, the star-shaped fort at the harbour mouth. This actually stands on the tiny Port Island and may not always be accessible.

Turn the headland and enjoy views across the sea to Mweelrea

A group of walkers on the northern cliffs of Inishbofin

and the Twelve Bens, with a spread of small islands. Pick a way along the rugged coast, staying well above the rocky shore, walking on grass or heather slopes. A couple of fences need to be crossed and there are two significant rocky gashes which appear quite suddenly and need to be passed on their upper sides. Later, a stony track can be followed to a sandy bay. Note the rugged islet of Inishlyon, linked to Inishbofin by a rocky bar at low tide. The view now extends beyond Mweelrea to embrace Croagh Patrick, the Nephins, Inishturk and Clare Island.

Walk round the sandy bay, but as there is a conservation scheme in operation you must leave by using a sandy track linking with a tarmac road. Follow the road left if a visit to St. Colman's Abbey is required, or straight onwards to regain the coast at East End Bay. A straggly line of low, whitewashed cottages curve around the bay. When the road turns inland, drop down to follow the beach onwards, aiming for a solitary white cottage, then come ashore. A grassy track rises beside the cottage, and once a gate has been passed, continue walking uphill beside a boundary wall. Follow the wall to the right, keeping above a couple of farms, to regain the rocky coast of the island.

Turn left to follow the coast, keeping well above the rocky shore. There are views across the sea to Inishturk and Achill Island. Watch out for an arch in the cliff, known as The Prison, then follow a route in and out, up and down, as the rugged headland is turned. There are fine stacks, and a deep inlet called Ardlea Cove. A fence needs to be crossed at the head of Bunnamullen Bay, and the route continues round the next headland, which has a rocky islet offshore. Continue around the indented cliff coast into the next bay, to reach North Beach.

There is a bar across the head of the bay, with Lough Bofin inland. Use a gate to gain access to the bar, then crunch along its pebbles. Continue along a coastal track, passing a handful of houses to reach another rugged, open headland. Keep to the right, aiming for the coast, but also looking for a large hole in the ground. Take a peep into the hole, which is a cave tunnel connected to the ocean. Heading over the tunnel to the sea, another broad gash in the rock will be passed, then a left turn leads along the cliff coast.

The grass is short and bare rock protrudes from the ground. Pass a bronze cross and climb in stages to reach the top of a large, grassy, cliff-bound dome overlooking Inishark. The dome bears a promontory fort and its rampart can be distinguished. A grassy track can be seen running back towards the harbour mouth on Inishbofin. At first it runs unenclosed, then later it becomes a narrow tarmac road passing a number of houses and the Doonmore Hotel. Simply follow the road as it snakes back through the village, passing white marker towers to lead walkers back to the pier.

St. Colman's Abbey

The Christian history of Inishbofin is a turbulent one. St. Colman arrived in the year 665, in a fury after the Synod of Whitby set new rules for the date of Easter. A monastery was founded by thirty monks, though the present ruins are of a 14th century church, which was used up to the 16th century. During Cromwell's time, priests were dispatched to places such as Inishbofin. Some were killed or transported, while others were imprisoned. The rock arch known as The Prison is said to have held several priests until 1660.

Cromwell's Fort

In terms of military history, Inishbofin is a significant island. Its long, natural, sheltered harbour did not go unnoticed through the ages. The O'Malleys held the island from 1380 to 1603, and the sea-queen Granuaile raided passing ships and mainland settlements. Don Bosco, a Spanish pirate and contemporary of Granuaile, built a fort at the mouth of the harbour. This is now occupied by Cromwell's Fort, which was built following the surrender of the island to Cromwell as late as 1653. The star-shaped fort had 24 cannons and even its crumbled ruins are an imposing sight.

WALK 29

Inishturk

Inishturk is a pig-in-the-middle island; smaller, quieter and less visited than its neighbours Inishbofin and Clare Island. Ferries can be irregular and in the depths of winter may be restricted to one run a week or less. The economy of the island is based on fishing and farming, and facilities for visitors are limited to a handful of B&Bs. In the summer months, it is usual for weekday ferries to run from Cleggan and weekend ferries from Roonagh Quay. A walk around the island could be accomplished between ferries, but it is better to stay overnight and make the most of the visit. There is an easy road walk, followed by a dramatic cliff coast walk to a ruined signal tower on the highest point of the island.

The Route

Distance:	6 miles (10 kilometres).
Start:	The Harbour, Inishturk - 620749.
Map:	OS Discovery Sheet 37.
Terrain:	A road walk, followed by pathless slopes and rugged cliffs.
Parking:	Cars cannot be taken to the island. Parking available at Cleggan and Roonagh Quay.
Transport:	Bus Eireann table number 419 serves Cleggan, while table number 450 runs to Louisburgh near Roonagh Quay. Irregular ferries serve Inishturk from Roonagh Quay and Cleggan.

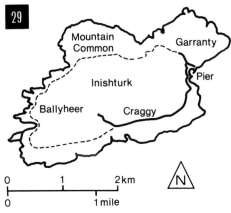

Leave the harbour on Inishturk by following the narrow road uphill from Harbour Lodge B&B, turning left beyond a phone box. The road climbs, enjoying views across the harbour to Caher Island, Clew Bay and Croagh Patrick, quickly embracing Mweelrea and the mountains of Connemara. The road rises past the island's electricity generator, Community Centre and St. Columba's National School. The road descends and there is a sign pointing right to Teach Abhainn B&B, while to the left a small pool can be seen beside the open sea. The road crosses a small river and rises. A gate on the left leads to a house, but go through another gate on the left to follow a track towards some more distant houses. Branch left of this track, passing through a gap in a wall, to walk towards the western end of the island. There is a sort of natural grassy groove flanked by little ridges of rock, and later you need to go through a gate in a wall. Keep to a high level and go west until the rugged coast is reached.

Don't descend all the way to the rocky shore, but turn right and keep fairly high. Ridges of rock and grassy slopes need to be negotiated, and there is a rocky gash which needs to be avoided before Dromore Head. Beyond Dromore Head, climb a rocky, grassy slope in stages, noting short lengths of wall and fencing which guard the precipitous cliffs on the western side of the island. There are a couple of jagged stacks, sheer rock walls and even some overhangs. Gradually drift away from the cliffs and climb further uphill, aiming for the highest point on Inishturk, which is crowned by the mouldering ruins of an old signal tower, with a trig point alongside at 629ft (191m). This is a superb viewpoint in clear weather, embracing Achill and Clare Island, through the Nephin Beg Range to Croagh Patrick and the Mountains of Connemara. Inishbofin completes the round.

The descent from the signal tower needs a little care. The course of an old track can be seen below, but there are steep slopes and rocky outcrops on the way. Pick up the track and follow it further along the rugged slopes above the sea. The track twists and turns, but generally leads downhill and passes through a gate in a wall. A patchy road runs downhill past a few houses, and a left turn leads back to the harbour. A little chapel stands just to the left of the harbour and a short length of track could be followed in this direction, but the eastern end of the island is rough and rocky.

WALK 30

Clare Island

Clare Island is easily recognised from the mainland or from other islands because of the huge hump of Knockmore, its highest hill. The island was the home of Granuaile, the sea-queen and pirate who harried the shipping lanes and mainland, and is believed to be buried in Clare Island Abbey. A walk around the island takes in the towering dome of Knockmore, as well as fine cliff walks, and the views are among the most extensive of any coastal walk, featuring ranges of mountains and a spread of islands.

The Route

Distance:	11 miles (18 kilometres).
Start:	At the pier beside Granuaile's Castle - 715853.
Map:	OS Discovery Sheet 30.
Terrain:	Some road walking, but also tracks and a rugged cliff walk.
Parking:	Cars cannot be taken to the island. Parking available at Roonagh Quay.
Transport:	Ferries run to Clare Island from Roonagh Pier near Louisburgh. Buses run no closer than Louisburgh.

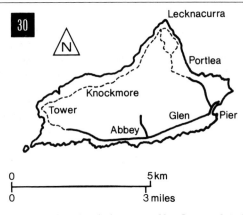

Start at the pier on the island, dominated by Granuaile's Castle, and follow the road inland, turning left at a junction by a telephone box. The road runs for a while without good views, then the mountains of Connemara can be seen across the sea. A shop and church are passed at another junction, where the ruined Clare Island Abbey stands, and where the grave of Granuaile may be located. Keep to the lower road, reaching O'Malley's B&B near the end of the tarmac. (It could be worth getting a lift from the pier to this point to avoid the initial road-walk.) Just opposite the B&B a track climbs uphill, passing one last house and reaching a large, open, overgrazed area above some remarkable cliffs. The cliff edge appears quite suddenly, so take care. Look out for choughs and fulmars soaring on the thermals.

Turn right to walk up to a ruined Signal Tower. Keep walking in the direction of Knockmore, climbing on short grass punctuated by a few boulders and low outcrops of rock. As height is gained, views become more extensive. The first summit is peaty, while the next is crowned by a huge cairn, but the highest bears a trig point at 1520ft (462m). Views stretch from Achill Head, through Achill Island, taking in North Mayo and the Nephins. Croaghmoyle and the distant Ox Mountains are followed by Croagh Patrick's towering cone. The Sheeffry Hills, Ben Gorm, Mweelrea, Twelve Bens and Errisbeg Mountain lead the eye back towards the sea. Peninsulas and small islands stretch to Inishturk and Inishbofin.

Walk downhill from Knockmore, noting the roller-coaster appearance of the cliff-line leading to the lighthouse at Lecknacurra. There are some steep, grassy slopes along the way, as well as outcropping rock needing care. Mostly, but not always, there is a fence along the line of the cliffs. On the lowest dip, cross a junction of fences and climb uphill again. Later, as the lighthouse draws near, there are fine views back along the cliffs to the towering dome of Knockmore. Cross the lighthouse access road and continue along the cliffs until a small harbour is reached. At this point, the coast ahead is cut by fences and walls, so follow a track inland to reach the lighthouse access road again. Turn left to follow this to a tarmac road, which passes through the small settlement of Maum on the way back to the pier. The Bay Hotel offers food and drink off to the left as soon as the coast is reached.

Granuaile
Where history is thin, folklore has been quick to flesh out the story of this notorious female pirate. While 'Granuaile' is a common spelling of her name, it has been presented in many forms and Anglicised as Grace O'Malley. It is a fact that she lived for over seventy years in the turbulent 16th century. It is a fact that she conducted pirate raids on shipping from her strongholds on Clare Island, Achill Island and Inishbofin. She held mainland castles and was equally adept at raiding on land. It is also a fact that she sailed to London and was granted a pardon from Queen Elizabeth I. She was even permitted to continue her piracy under the guise of harrying the queen's enemies! She was a formidable woman, overshadowing her husbands and being most adept at handling the political turmoil of the times. It is believed that she is buried in the Abbey on Clare Island; a place noted for its wall paintings.

Clare Island Survey
Between the years 1909-1911, Clare Island was the subject of a monumental survey by a team of academics and natural historians. Comprehensive lists of plants and animals, as well as archaeological sites, are interspersed with comments and stories taken from the islanders of the time. The results of the survey were published in a weighty tome, which many islanders possess. In the introduction it

is stated: 'The selection of Clare Island was influenced by its suitable size, position and unusual elevation as compared with most of the western islands; it lay sufficiently off the coast to raise interesting problems as to the immigration of its flora and fauna, but not so far as to introduce delay and expense to the working parties owing to precarious communication with the mainland.'

WALK 31

Minaun Cliffs

The Minaun Cliffs present a dramatic sight when seen from Keel and Pollagh at the western end of Achill Island, and an approach could be made from the broad sweep of Keel Strand. However, walkers will notice a couple of tall masts on top of the Minaun Heights, and these are served by a road from the other side. A circular walk based on Dooega starts with a road walk to the Minaun Heights, followed by a fine cliff walk to Dooega Head and a final descent back to the village of Dooega. Walkers relying on bus services could adapt the walk to start and finish at Cashel.

The Route

Distance:	11 miles (18 kilometres).
Start:	Lavelle's Seaside House, Dooega - 675994.
Map:	OS Discovery Sheet 30.
Terrain:	Road walking all the way uphill, followed by a cliff walk with intermittent paths which need care in mist.
Parking:	Lavelle's Seaside House, Dooega.
Transport:	Bus Eireann table numbers 66, 69, 440 & 441 could be used by walkers starting from Cashel.

Walkers relying on bus services to and from Achill can easily adapt this walk to start and finish at Ted Lavelle's Lounge Bar at Cashel, and the Minaun Heights are signposted from a nearby road junction. A car park is available at Lavelle's Seaside House at Dooega, which could be used by anyone availing of accommodation at the pub, otherwise ask for permission. Food and drink are on hand at this point, and the bar is a good reference point in a village of scattered

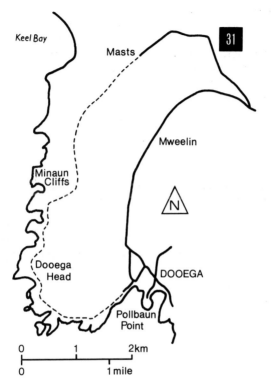

Keel Bay

Masts

31

Mweelin

Minaun
Cliffs

N

Dooega
Head

DOOEGA

Pollbaun
Point

0   1   2km

0   1 mile

housing and narrow unsignposted roads.

Walk downhill and turn right by road after passing a telephone
box. At the next junction, keep straight on and follow the road as it
crosses Dooega River and bears right to climb gradually up through
a broad valley. Numerous farms and houses are passed around
Mweelin, then these eventually give way to an extensive area of bog
with abundant turf cuttings. At the top of the road, on a broad and
boggy gap, a turning to the left is signposted for the Minaun
Heights. Follow the road uphill as it slices across the hillside. It is
accompanied by telegraph poles at a higher level, and views open
up dramatically in clear weather. The road leads to a parking space

beside a tall mast, and a track leads to another tall mast, followed by a couple of smaller masts. Thankfully, the highest part of the hill has been spared such intrusions and can be reached by following a stony path up a heathery slope. The top of the Minaun Heights is crowned by a stout cairn and a statue of the Blessed Virgin.

Pause for a while to absorb the extensive view. The jagged crest of Benmore is followed by the towering heights of Croaghaun and Slievemore, with the wave-washed Keel Strand far below. The Belmullet peninsula and cliffs of North Mayo give way to the broad humps of the Nephin Beg Range. Try and figure out where Achill Island ends and the mainland at Corraun begins, as little hills obscure the narrow channel. Croagh Patrick and Mweelrea give way to the rugged Twelve Bens and the mountains of Connemara. Neighbouring islands include Clare Island, Inishturk and distant Inishbofin.

Continue along the crest of the Minaun Heights, passing a rash of cairns before starting a steep descent. Walking on short heather liberally laced with creeping juniper and bearberry, avoid a large patch of stones by keeping to the right, but swing left as marked by a couple of cairns to reach a heathery gap. There is a vague path on the gap, but this is lost in a boggy area on the next gentle ascent. On top of this unassuming rise, magnificent cliff views begin to develop. Short stretches of path can be followed from one heathery rise to another, and there are chances to peep over the edge to note sloping and sheer rock walls, and even overhanging cliffs. Later, a couple of rugged stacks can be seen from Dooega Head.

When a length of ruined wall is followed downhill, there is a chance to cut off to the left and descend a steep slope of short heather to reach another ruined wall at the bottom. Turn left to follow a path alongside the wall, ending at a narrow, rocky inlet. Walk across an area of bog to reach a track, and follow this towards the first few buildings in Dooega. Note the rampant growths of 'elephant rhubarb' which have assumed pest proportions on the island. When a road junction is reached, turn right to cross Dooega River, then right again at the next junction. A left turn leads past the phone box to return to Lavelle's Seaside House, food and drink.

WALK 32
Croaghaun & Achill Head

Ireland's highest sea cliffs aren't on the mainland, but are out on the jagged western end of Achill Island. Here, Croaghaun's shattered, stony slopes fall 2200ft (670m) into the Atlantic Ocean. Anyone contemplating an ascent should note that there are some very steep slopes to be negotiated, and this is not a walk to be attempted in wet, windy or misty weather. An added bonus on a fine day is Achill Head, which is a rugged spine of rock projecting out into the ocean. A walk out onto the headland has to be reversed afterwards, as there is simply nowhere else to go!

The Route

Distance:	16 miles (26 kilometres).
Start:	Dooagh - 605049.
Map:	OS Discovery Sheet 30.
Terrain:	Some tracks and paths, but also rugged moorland and plenty of rock. Some slopes are very steep. The route ends with some road walking.
Parking:	Beside Dooagh Strand in the village.
Transport:	Bus Eireann table numbers 66, 69, 440 & 441 serve Dooagh.

Dooagh is the last village on the road west across Achill Island. It is also the terminus for Bus Eireann services and cars can be parked overlooking the strand. Start walking near the post office and follow a minor road which passes the Atlantic Hotel. The tarmac peters out and a pebbly track rises gently uphill, passing a few fields and extensive turf cuttings. On the crest of this track, the huge dome of Slievemore rises ahead and the ruins of a long-deserted village can be seen along its lower slopes. Turn left, however, to start walking towards the higher hill of Croaghaun, crossing turf cuttings and climbing up a small, heathery hill. The summit stands at 645ft (194m) and is crowned by the ruins of an old signal tower.

Head west from the tower to cross a gentle gap, and climb up another heathery slope to gain a summit at 891ft (269m). There are fine views of Lough Nakeeroge perched above Annagh Strand.

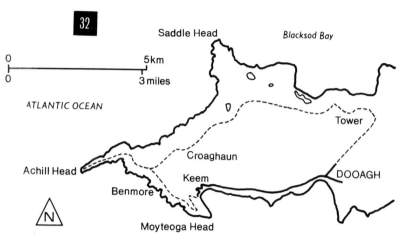

Walk south-west to avoid outcropping rock, cross another gentle gap and another little summit. Heather gives way to grass on the descent to a broad, boggy gap overlooking Lough Nakeeroge. A steep, heathery slope is peppered with boulders and eventually gives way to a broad, boggy, grassy shoulder. There are pools of water on the shoulder, followed by stony ground. Turn left when a steep, rocky edge is reached, enjoying fine views into the coum holding Bunnatreva Lough West.

As the ascent continues, be careful of deeply fissured ground where immense slabs of rock must surely one day peel from the face of the mountain and crash into the ocean. A final steep, heathery, bouldery slope leads to the top of Croaghaun. A cairn stands on the summit at 2260ft (688m) and the sea is wrapped around three sides of the view. Enjoy the remarkable spread of islands and mountains from Belmullet and the Nephins to Clew Bay and Croagh Patrick, with Clare Island, Inishturk and Inishbofin backed by the mountains of Connemara.

There is a clear path trodden along a narrow ridge linking two summits on Croaghaun. The main summit is followed by a subsidiary summit at 2192ft (664m). Beyond this more pointed summit there is a sustained loss of height. The ground steepens rapidly and should be taken slowly and steadily, zigzagging around boulders on areas of heather. On the lower slopes there is more grass and fewer boulders. A boggy valley bottom is reached just to the right of a couple of little loughs. Climb straight uphill to reach the jagged crest of Benmore at 1098ft (332m). A decision needs to be made at this point. A left turn for Keem Strand allows the route to be shortened, while a right turn takes in Achill Head, but requires steps to be retraced afterwards.

If Achill Head is to be visited, then there is a significant grassy saddle to cross, followed by knobbly, rocky humps leading towards the end of the point. Walk as far as you want, then turn around and walk back over Benmore. There is a path which allows the rugged little tops of Benmore to be omitted, but anyone including them will have much better views of the awesome cliffs on this part of the walk. Some parts even overhang. The final top is crowned by a lookout tower and is known as Moyteoga Head. Steps need to be retraced a little from the tower, unless you took the opportunity to start the descent earlier. The path leads down to Keem Strand where there is a car park and information board overlooking a fine little sandy beach.

A simple road walk leads back from Keem Strand to Dooagh. Start by zigzagging uphill from the beach, passing toilets and a higher car park. The road slices across the steep and rugged flanks of Croaghaun and enjoys fine coastal views as it rises. When the road starts to descend, look out for the word 'EIRE' spelt in stones on a coastal heath, which was intended to warn Second World War aircraft not to land in neutral Ireland. The scattered white buildings of Dooagh offer food and drink as the walk draws to a close. A commemorative stone records the arrival of Don Allum; the only man ever to have rowed both ways across the Atlantic Ocean. The pub across the road has photographs and information about the landing. The post office where the walk started is a little further along the road.

WALK 33

Benwee Head

Tucked away in a remote part of North Mayo, Benwee Head is seldom seen at close quarters. Its majestic cliffs, rugged headlands, rocky coves and jagged stacks are apparent only to those who will walk to discover them. Empty bog roads serve the settlements of Portacloy and Carrowteige, where only limited services are available. This is a connoisseur's cliff walk; and one which walkers with an interest in geology, photography or ornithology will take at a slow pace. The circuit described leads from Portacloy, over Benwee Head and round to Carrowteige, closing with a road-walk through a broad bog.

The Route

Distance:	12 miles (20 kilometres).
Start:	Portacloy Bay - 840440.
Maps:	OS Discovery Sheets 22 & 23.
Terrain:	Easy walking on short grass and steep slopes. The last stretch is along roads.
Parking:	Limited small spaces around Portacloy.
Transport:	Bus Eireann services run no nearer than Ballycastle and Bangor Erris. A local minibus service is operated by McGrath's Coaches.

Start on the bridge over the river at the head of Portacloy Bay, and follow the road uphill above the bay. Pass above two concrete slipways to reach the end of the road, then continue through a small gate in a fence. Cross over a stream and follow a vague path across a slope of short grass and heather. The path leads to a little concrete hut out on a point, where there are fine views along the cliffs and out to the Stags of Broadhaven. Retrace steps, noting the word 'EIRE' laid out in huge stone letters, then climb uphill to the right. As you turn around a rock-walled cove, note the cliff-girt headland which features the remains of a promontory fort. It appears to be accessible only to rock-climbers, but was obviously ideally situated for defence. Looking inland, Portacloy is seen as a scattering of houses and farms

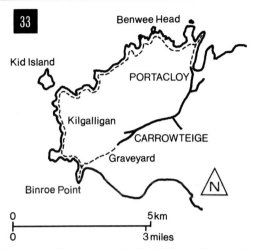

in a broad, green valley surrounded by hills and brown bog.

The next rocky bay features sloping cliffs cut into angular, geometric forms which are quite remarkable. As you walk round the bay, short lengths of fencing steer you away from some crumbling edges. Later, looking back, the cliffs display some quite striking zigzag folding, with a series of caves along their bases. A two-pronged jagged rock protruding from the rocky cove is a notable feature on the ascent of the next grassy hump. Walk downhill, crossing a gap which could be a bit wet and squelchy, overlooking pyramidal stacks and a jagged headland pierced with a hole. On the next ascent, further holes can be seen on the other side of the headland. A fence steers walkers away from the cliff edge on the highest part of Benwee Head. The summit is covered with blanket bog and rises to 829ft (255m).

From Benwee Head, the eye is drawn along a cliff-line washed by a sea which is spiky with rocky stacks, with Kid Island's gentle crest rising beyond. Following the cliff edge involves walking out onto a series of headlands and turning round rocky coves in between. The first headland and cove lead to a road-end, which offers rapid access inland if required. A turf bank runs parallel to the cliffs, and the walk appears to be heading for a distant grassy hill.

The hill is in fact Kid Island, and so a left turn around the headland is made without reaching that point. There are some fine rocky stacks between the headland and the island.

The turf bank leads straight onwards, and following its course offers the easiest means of progression. Walking seawards of the bank allows little headlands to be explored, but the walk becomes more of a roller-coaster. A significant steep-sided little river valley needs to be crossed, then the turf bank climbs straight uphill. At the top, bear right to head out onto a final rugged point and turn left around its end. The turf bank makes its own left turn earlier. Either way, walk along a lower cliff-line overlooking Broad Haven. There is one point where a fence runs rather near the cliff edge, but the field it encloses can be entered and left using little gates on the top side. A sandy, grassy slope leads down to a sandy bay and a narrow tarmac road. The road can be used to explore Rinroe Point, with steps being retraced afterwards, but there is only a ruin and a little harbour in that direction.

After crossing the narrow road, a track can be followed across the sandy, grassy common to reach a graveyard at the foot of a hill crowned by the houses of Stonefield. The graveyard features an ancient cairn and a more modern Marian shrine. Follow a narrow, fenced, tarmac road uphill and keep straight on past a junction. The road is accompanied by trees and bushes, which have been absent around the cliffs, and there are a few houses. At the top of the road, turn right to pass a telephone box, knitwear factory and shop at Carrowteige. The village sits on a gap and the road runs straight downhill across a broad bog. Walk straight through a road junction at the bottom to return to Portacloy. Anyone staying overnight can use a B&B called Stag View which overlooks Portacloy Bay.

WALK 34

Belderrig to Portacloy

The cliff walk from Belderrig to Portacloy is like a monstrous roller-coaster. In effect, a range of hills lie between the two settlements; their northern slopes broken by cliffs pounded by the Atlantic and their southern slopes stretching into immense boglands. This area is only thinly scored by roads, sparsely settled, with a limited local minibus service. The cliff walk is linear and has a B&B at either end, with a shop selling food and drink off-centre at Porturlin. Anyone looking for a sustained weekend of cliff walking can tie this walk with the walk around Benwee Head.

The Route

Distance:	15 miles (24 kilometres).
Start:	Belderrig - 993396.
Finish:	Portacloy Bay - 840440.
Map:	OS Discovery Sheet 23.
Terrain:	Plenty of ascents and descents, with some steep slopes. Grassy and heathery, with some boggy patches.
Parking:	There is only limited roadside parking at Belderrig and Portacloy.
Transport:	Bus Eireann services run no closer than Ballycastle. A local minibus service is operated by McGrath's Coaches.

Belderrig is a small, scattered village between Ballycastle and Belmullet. Walk downhill from the First Fence grocery store and turn right along a minor road signposted for a B&B, camping, boat trips, pony and trap rides, Pre-historic Farm Site, etc. The road runs down past a school, then a left turn uphill is signposted for the Yellow Rose B&B. The Pre-historic Farm Site is just to the left at a crossroads, otherwise continue uphill to pass the B&B. If your walk starts from the Yellow Rose B&B, then you can save the first $1^{1/2}$ miles (2 kilometres) of walking.

Beyond the Yellow Rose there are a few more houses, then the tarmac road ends on a broad and boggy slope. There are bog roads, but these do not lead to the cliffs. Head off to the right, across an area of rugged, wet, cutaway bog. There are some squelchy patches of sphagnum moss amid the grass and heather, while a little creeping juniper can be spotted on the way up a prominent heathery hill. From this first hill, there are fine views along the coast from Downpatrick Head to Glinsk and out to the Stags of Broadhaven. The mountains of Donegal may feature across the sea on a very clear day. Rolling hills and broad bogs stretch inland to the huge humps of the Nephin Beg Range. Descend to a grassy gap and climb up the next grassy rise. A broad, grass and heather descent leads to a turf bank, which is a good feature to follow even if it is a step back from the cliffs. The bank drops to cross a little river, then climbs alongside a fence. There is a narrow, rocky chasm off to the right, with a rocky arch at its far end. Cross a fence and continue climbing, or turn right to follow the fence round the cliffs. Either way, the broad top of Glinsk will be reached. Rugged, boggy moorlands feature heather,

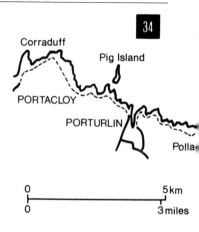

bare peat and some stony patches. The fence turns a corner to reach the 1002ft (304m) summit, but there is no need to go all the way.

The western slopes of Glinsk are steep and rugged in places. Keep away from the cliffs, but also keep away from the forests further inland. Cross a little gap and walk over another heathery rise, then descend steeply again, noting creeping willow in the heather. There are fine views of the green humped sea stack of Illanmaster, severed from the mainland cliffs by a narrow chasm. A gap is crossed where there is a very narrow, rock-walled cove. Cross a fence, then follow the fence as it clings to a steep slope on the next ascent. The fence runs close to the 780ft (238m) summit of the hill, then descends along the cliff edge with fine views onwards. Rugged headlands and bays stretch all the way to Benwee Head. The fence turns around the head of a narrow chasm where fulmars can be observed, then there is a junction of fences further down the close-cropped grassy slope. Walk across a broad gap and note the isolated ruined farmstead at Laghtmurragha.

After rising to a junction of fences, climb up a rugged, heathery slope and continue along a cliff edge with no fence. The ground is rough and boggy, and the descent needs a little thought and care. It is best to keep well inland from the cliffs, walking across a rolling moorland, then descending into a narrow little valley at Pollagh.

The steep slope down into the valley is covered with heather, bracken and stony patches. The climb out of the valley is simply steep and heathery. Look out for a sudden, narrow, rocky chasm which frames a distant view of the Stags of Broadhaven. Continue along an undulating grass and heather crest, noting that the cliffs actually overhang further along. Towards the end, the cliff-line turns and allows a fine view of rocky stacks and headlands stretching back towards Illanmaster, and forwards to Pig Island and the Stags of Broadhaven. Inland, distant hills and mountains are seen stretching from Achill Island through the Nephin Beg Range.

Descend towards the narrow inlet at Porturlin. A fence steers you leftwards towards a small group of houses, and their access road can be followed far inland across a bog. Turn right to follow a road across a river, then right again to walk through Porturlin. There is a small shop and phone box on the way to the pier. The inlet could of course be crossed quite easily when the tide is out, saving the road-walk inland and through the village, cutting 1¹/₂ miles (2 kilometres) off the total distance.

Follow a narrow road above the pier, aiming for a house at the end which is marked as 'Sliogéisc Phort-Urlinn'. Crabs are packed here and there may be a fishy smell on the breeze. Just before reaching the house, go through a gate on the left and walk across a field. A narrow, fenced path leads up to a small gate, which leads onto an open slope near the cliffs. Either follow an old turf bank uphill, or walk alongside the fence near the cliff edge. There are fine views back along the cliff coast, but it is difficult to appreciate the nearby cliffs properly.

The slope levels out in a broad and boggy area. In fact, there are three broad, boggy rises stretching into the distance, and a route needs to be chosen with care. Walking near the cliff edge leads onto rugged ground, with lots of little ups and downs. Walking too far inland leads onto rugged peat hags. Walking in between is easiest, crossing a slope of heather and squelchy cotton grass. There is a gradual swing round to the left, with a view over the mouth of Portacloy Bay and Benwee Head. Follow the cliff edge until it is possible to see down a steep slope to the scattered settlement of Portacloy. Walk down towards the nearest farm, crossing only one low fence and passing through gates into the farmyard. This is the Stag View B&B, which offers evening meals, and if no other arrangements have been made to be collected, then this is a fine place to end.

Belderrig Pre-historic Farm Site
The field walls at this site are thought to be Neolithic, contemporaneous with the nearby Ceide Fields, with the addition of Bronze Age monuments. Copper ore deposits have been found on the nearby Horse Island. The central feature of the site is a Bronze Age circular house with a paved entrance, door jambs and threshold, as well as a hearth stone, external wall and roof supports. Three tillage plots are located at the back, where wheat and barley would have been grown.

Porturlin and Portacloy
During the years of the Great Famine, Richard Webb toured this part of Ireland and reported back to the Society of Friends. After visiting Porturlin he wrote: 'The only access by land is over a high and boggy mountain so wet and swampy that it is difficult to reach it even in Summer. There is probably not in Ireland a cluster of human habitations so completely secluded from easy access.' Noting the nature of the coast and the dearth of safe harbours, he wrote: 'For about ten miles the only ports are the coves of Portacloy and Porturlin, and even these are not easily gained when a heavy swell sets in.' Between 1846 and 1910 piers, roads and bridges were constructed piecemeal in the area, yet the communities are still isolated between the sea and broad tracts of bog.

WALK 35

Downpatrick Head

The walk around Downpatrick Head near Ballycastle is very short, in fact, the shortest in this book, but it abounds in interest. The cliffs are mostly undercut and feature numerous caves, and the sea has cut a subterranean passageway through the headland. Offshore is a tall, layered sea stack called Dún Briste which, along with the cliff faces, has abundant ledges for a range of nesting birds. A deep, square-cut blowhole in the centre of the headland has a rather grisly history.

The Route

Distance:	¹/₂ mile (1 kilometre).
Start:	Downpatrick Head car park - 125424.
Map:	OS Discovery Sheet 23.
Terrain:	Easy walking on short grass, but the cliffs overhang and need care.
Parking:	Just behind Downpatrick Head.
Transport:	Bus Eireann table number 445 serves nearby Ballycastle.

A series of minor roads lead from Ballycastle to Downpatrick Head, and there is a parking space at the end of the final patchy road. Note the strange stone sculpture near the end of the road, which is part of the Tír Sáile Sculpture Trail. There are picnic tables overlooking a rocky shore. A trodden path leads through three gateways and

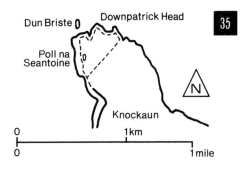

One of the blow-holes which punctuate the headland

two fields to reach a sign reading: 'This is a Natural Heritage Area. Warning. You are entering at your own risk a recreational area which has dangerous overhanging cliffs and blowholes. Children must be accompanied by an adult. No vehicles past this point. 1995 Occupiers Act applies.' It all sounds very stern and forbidding, but in fact the headland is fascinating.

Walk up to a fenced-off blowhole, which has a stone block inscribed: 'To the memory of the people of Knockaun and Killeen who lost their lives here in Poll na Seantoine in the aftermath of the Rebellion of 1798.' The inscription is repeated in French. Looking into the blowhole, the sea can be seen slopping around inside, and the subterranean channel actually connects with the sea on the north and west side of the headland. Further uphill from the blowhole is a statue of St. Patrick inside the walls of a ruined church, then there is an old concrete lookout perched near the edge of the cliff.

The cliffs are undercut, so tread carefully. The tall stack of Dún Briste rises offshore and is slightly higher than the rest of the headland. Turn left to walk round an overhanging rim of cliffs, where the sea works its way through the headland from one side to the other. The grass on the headland is speckled with thrift, which forms soft cushions on the highest cliffs. Keep walking round the next couple of headlands, marvelling at the layered strata, often occupied by fulmars and stained with bird-lime. Look at the sea pounding into caves along the foot of the cliffs, and enjoy the more distant coastal views. A fence can be followed back across the headland, and the path leads back to the car park.

Downpatrick Head

St. Patrick is said to have driven all the snakes out of Ireland, and the last one went over the edge at Downpatrick Head! There is an ancient church ruin on the headland dedicated to St. Patrick. The stack of Dún Briste was once joined to the headland by a rock arch, and a few people lived in cottages on that exposed point. The arch collapsed one day, leaving the people stranded on top of the newly-formed stack. Escape was made possible by weaving the thatch from the cottage roofs into straw ropes, then climbing down to curraghs waiting to rescue them in the sea below. After the French landed at Killala, and were subsequently defeated in 1798, captives were thrown to their deaths at Poll na Seantoine.

Tír Sáile

Anyone travelling the roads between Ballina and Belmullet, linking the three coastal walks on the North Mayo Coast, will see the words 'Tír Sáile' on several signposts. They point the way to over a dozen sculptures which have been fashioned from rock, earth or other materials. The one near the car park on Downpatrick Head is called Battling Forces and 'gives form to a frozen moment in an ongoing struggle between two forces of a different nature.'

WALK 36

Slieve League

One of the most popular cliff coast scenes in Ireland can be approached by following a narrow road from Carrick to Teelin and Bunglass. The rugged slopes falling from Slieve League into the

Atlantic Ocean present the viewer with a colourful, chaotic scene for minimal effort. William Allingham, the Ballyshanny Poet, spoke of 'That ocean-mountain steep; six hundred yards in air aloft, six hundred in the deep.' Walkers can literally get to grips with Slieve League by following a skyline route involving a short scramble along a knife-edge of rock. Of course, it's possible to avoid this highlight, but the walk is still quite rough and rocky. A descent can be made inland, tracing a pilgrimage path down through a wild glen, closing the circuit with a road walk back to Bunglass.

The Route

Distance:	9 miles (15 kilometres).
Start:	Bunglass, near Teelin - 558757.
Map:	OS Discovery Sheet 10.
Terrain:	Mostly on well-worn paths, tracks and roads, but some parts can be steep and rocky. There is an optional short scramble along a rocky ridge.
Parking:	At the end of the road at Bunglass.
Transport:	Bus Eireann table number 490 runs through nearby Carrick.

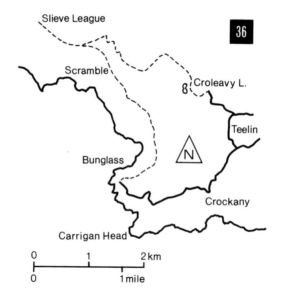

Slieve League is signposted from Carrick, but the signposts lead to a small car park on an old pilgrim path to the summit. Don't travel this way, but continue through Teelin and follow the road signposted for Bunglass and the cliffs. The tarmac ends at another small car park on a cliff edge, where a sweeping view embraces the rugged sea slopes of Slieve League. They call this place Radharc Mor, or the Big View. An awesome, rugged face of broken rock, bracken and heather drops nearly 2000ft (600m) into the Atlantic. Be sure to walk there in clear weather to make the most of the wonderful scenery. The route is fairly obvious, sticking closely to the skyline to reach the summit.

A trodden path accompanies a fence uphill from the car park. The fence soon ends, but the path continues climbing up a rough and rocky slope to reach a summit called Scregeighter. Swing to the left to follow a cliff path roughly northwards, but walk well away from the edge while crossing the next rise, where there are overhangs around the Eagle's Nest. The path crosses a gap and rises over a hump. The boggy, heathery ground is eroded in places and the path is becoming braided. Climb steeply uphill and either cross or pass another hump on the crest. The ground becomes steep and rocky and a decision needs to be made.

The rocky ridge of Keeringear has become known as the One Man's Pass in recent years, though this name strictly applies to a feature further along the route. The ridge is steeply pitched and quite sharp, requiring the use of hands and a good head for heights. In wet weather the rock could be slippery, while in windy weather it is best avoided. The hardest move involves actually getting onto the ridge, and if that can be accomplished, the ascent can be covered on all fours, with the Atlantic Ocean down to the left and a rugged glen down to the right. At the top end, cross a rocky notch and keep to the right of the ridge to continue uphill. A simple but spectacular scramble. Cautious walkers can omit the entire scramble, and will find a rough, trodden path on the glenward side of the ridge. Either way, a path runs out onto the broad top of Slieve League.

The wide, stony plateau is not actually the true summit of Slieve League, which is actually further away to the north-west. The two broad summits are connected by a narrow ridge, which is the true One Man's Pass. The ridge bears a path and is quite straightforward, being nothing like the previous scramble. A short, steep, rocky climb at the end leads to the summit plateau, where there is a large cairn. The map marks a trig point at 1972ft (595m), but if this is present it must be buried inside the cairn! In clear weather it should be possible to see in an arc from Arranmore Island, through the mountains of Donegal, Leitrim, Sligo and Mayo, to the distant cliffs of Benwee Head and Achill Island.

Steps need to be retraced along the ridge linking the two broad summits. On the way across the lower summit, swing to the left, walking roughly north-east down a stony slope. There are cairns and the ruins of crude shelters, some of which are associated with an old pilgrimage route. Look out for a clear, worn path which descends into a wild glen. This drops steeply at first, then becomes more gently graded. The path becomes a fine track, with substantial buttressing, crossing a stream beside some fine waterfalls. The track passes the little Croleavy Lough and reaches a small car park.

Follow a narrow road downhill from the car park and turn right at a junction with another narrow road beside a bridge. This road has a wide strip of grass down its middle and sees very little traffic. It climbs uphill, then later falls to a junction with another road, where a right turn is made. You should recognise this as the road which was followed earlier in the day from Teelin, on the drive to Bunglass and the cliffs. The road twists and turns uphill, passing a few houses and going through a gate. As the road loops around Carrigan Head, note the word 'EIRE' spelt out in stones on the headland. The road leads back to the car park on the cliffs at Bunglass, where the walk started.

Slieve League Pilgrimage

The ascent of Slieve League used to be one of the most important pilgrimages in Ireland, but its popularity has waned over the past century. Slieve League is associated with St. Assicus, who was St. Patrick's goldsmith, and who is reputed to have lived on top of the mountain for seven years. The crumbled ruins of an oratory and a holy well are lost among sundry heaps of stones on the lower summit.

'EIRE'

Marks such as this are found at odd intervals all around the north-western coast of Ireland. They were laid out during the Second World War to warn warplane pilots not to land in neutral Ireland. Even landing in an emergency, or surviving a crash-landing, pilots were liable to be interned, and Donegal was frequently mistaken for Northern Ireland by misplaced navigators. Allied warplanes, however, were accustomed to use a 'secret air corridor' from Donegal Bay to Lower Lough Erne in Co. Fermanagh.

WALK 37
Glencolmcille

Tough walkers can enjoy a tough coastal walk from Maghera to Glencolmcille along the rugged northern side of the Carrick peninsula. Note that there are no facilities along the way, and that only the road serving Port allows the walk to be abandoned easily. For most of the way, the route uses sheep paths across rugged slopes of grass, heather and bog. Towards the end, astounding cliff scenery can be enjoyed, while Glencolmcille itself is a delightful place to explore. The route is structured so that a lift is necessary to reach Maghera, while Glencolmcille offers accommodation, shops, pubs and a bus service.

The Route

Distance:	16 miles (26 kilometres).
Start:	Maghera - 662907.
Finish:	Glencolmcille - 532846.
Map:	OS Discovery Sheet 10.
Terrain:	Rugged slopes of grass and heather, sometimes boggy, with paths often vague or absent.
Parking:	There is a small car park at Maghera, with more parking available around Glencolmcille.
Transport:	Bus Eireann table number 492 serves Ardara, near Maghera, and table number 490 serves Glencolmcille.

Buses serve Ardara, but don't run to Maghera. A lift to Maghera could be organised and there is a small car park among the little huddle of houses, where a signpost points to Maghera Strand and Caves. If you intend to walk along the strand to see the caves, then it's best to retrace steps afterwards, rather than attempt to climb straight uphill from the shore. There are sand dunes covered in spiky marram grass, and a fence can be followed uphill, crossing grassy hills which become more rugged with rock and heather as height is gained. At the top corner of the fence, keep climbing uphill, but also look out for any useful sheep paths cutting off to the right, overlooking Loughros Beg Bay. Aim to keep below Lough

Acruppan. Any further uphill and inland and you might as well climb Slievetooey!

A fairly prominent sheep path might be spotted, running across a huge heathery hollow, crossing a river and climbing over a boggy shoulder near the little Lough Beg. Descend a rough and boggy slope, crossing another river, with views of mountains to one side and the sea to the other. The sea is getting rather distant, so follow a grassy, boggy slope down towards a confluence of rivers closer to the cliffs. Cross the river and climb uphill to reach a cliff edge overlooking the blocky, rocky Gull Island. A steep and grassy slope gradually eases to become heathery and bouldery. The heather is laced with abundant creeping juniper and bearberry. Continue across an adjacent moorland hump, then drift to the right, rather than climbing any further. The course of an old stone wall can be followed across a steep slope overlooking the cliffs. After crossing the highest part of the cliffs, around 1000ft (300m), there are views further along the coast, as well as inland to Slieve League.

Birdwatching at the western end of Rathlin Island

Island, or at the harbour at Burtonport.

Transport: Lough Swilly buses serve Burtonport, from where there are regular daily ferries to Arranmore from Burtonport.

After landing at the pier on Arranmore Island, turn left and keep left by road, passing a couple of B&Bs and cafes. A signpost points left for Aphort Strand, passing a post office and Phil Bán's Bar & Shop. The road climbs to the right at a school, then there is a road to the left signposted for Pally's Bar. Take this turning if you still need refreshment, otherwise keep going straight onwards to pass Neily's Bar. There is a dip in the road, where a river is crossed, then the road rises and falls to reach O'Donnell's Atlantic Bar. Climb uphill again, passing the last few houses on the road. At the last house, zigzag further uphill to the right, along a broad, clear track. This leads from slopes of short grass onto an area of rock, boulders, bog and heather. The scene is suddenly quite bleak and barren.

The track runs up to a small quarry, but just before that point there is another track branching off to the left. Follow this track as it twists and turns, rises and falls on the rugged slopes. You could descend towards the cliffs at any time and follow them onwards. There is already a view of some of the cliffs, as well as the rounded

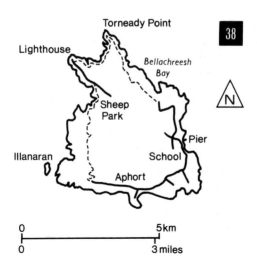

Boats drawn up in a bay on the gentle side of Arranmore

hump of Illanaran, or Green Island. There is a track branching to the right, which should be avoided, but turn left at the next junction. A track rises over a little gap, then descends and expires on the slope. Descend further to reach the cliffs and turn right to follow them onwards. The cliff tops are covered in short grass and offer easy walking. A number of slender waterfalls can be observed tumbling down to the sea, and these can become quite attractive after heavy rain. When a narrow tarmac road is reached, turn left to follow it down to a lighthouse at the end of the road. Enjoy the views back along the cliffs and away to the more distant Carrick peninsula and Slieve League.

Turn right to follow the enclosure wall away from the lighthouse, and climb up a grassy slope along the top of the cliffs. Spiky stacks fill rocky coves, and as height is gained the view extends from Tory Island and Bloody Foreland inland to Tievealehid, Muckish, Errigal, Slieve Snaght and other ranges of hills. There is a fence cutting across part of the headland, but step across it to see more of the dramatic cliff scenery, especially the towering stack called the Giant's Reek.

Turn around Torneady Point and walk across a slope above a less dramatic cliff line. Cross a heathery slope and look ahead to spot a huge boulder lying on the moorland slope above the cliffs. Follow a track inland from the boulder, reaching a junction with another track. Turn left to walk downhill across the rugged slope, enjoying wide-ranging views in clear weather. The track leads down to a narrow road serving a few farmhouses. Turn right to follow the road, and keep right at other junctions until a climb uphill leads past a couple of B&Bs to a road junction at a bridge. Turn left and walk downhill passing the Glen Hotel and Early's Bar, turning left again at the bottom to return to the pier.

Arranmore Way
The Arranmore Way is a series of three waymarked loop walks around the island. Two of the walks are quite short and are confined to the populated side of the island. The third is longer and makes use of the tracks and bog roads extending onto the higher parts of the island. None of the waymarked walks ventures close to the cliffs.

WALK 39

Bloody Foreland

Bloody Foreland is a significant corner on the coast of Co Donegal, backed by a whaleback heathery hill of the same name. A walk over the hill offers fine views along the coast, and inland to the mountains, then the coast itself can be followed using a series of tracks and paths around the edge of a broad bog. The circuit can be based on the scattered village of Knockfola, which offers a little accommodation and has a bus service. This is likely to be a quiet walk where you'll see only the local people.

The Route

Distance:	8¹/₂ miles (14 kilometres).
Start:	Knockfola - 818324.
Map:	OS Discovery Sheet 1.
Terrain:	Some tracks and paths, but also pathless hillsides.
Parking:	Roadside parking above Knockfola.
Transport:	Lough Swilly Buses run around Bloody Foreland serving Meenacloy, Knockfola and Brinlack.

The Ocean Lodge B&B at Knockfola makes a handy starting point. It is situated on a bendy stretch of the R257 road above the village and has a bus service. Cars can be parked at the top of the road. A farm access road passes Ocean Lodge, but leave it almost immediately to follow a fence across a moorland slope. There is a vague track alongside the fence, then a gate on top offers access to the heathery slopes rising to the left. Climb straight uphill, enjoying widening views and passing a cairn on a grassy, stony hump. Continue towards the top of the hill, noting how the heather is laced with crowberry and bearberry. There are rashes of stones on the way and parallel lines of stones mark the course of an old path to the summit. A large cairn and trig point on top stand at 1038ft (314m), surrounded by other cairns. Views extend to Tory Island, Inishbofin, Horn Head, Melmore Head, Inishowen, Muckish, the Aghlas, Errigal, Slieve Snaght, the Carrick peninsula, Arranmore Island and other little islands, ending with the point of Bloody Foreland at the foot of

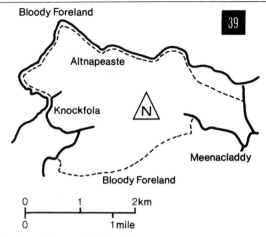

Bloody Foreland

39

Altnapeaste

Knockfola

N

Meenacladdy

Bloody Foreland

| 0 | 1 | 2km |
| 0 | | 1 mile |

the hill, where this walk is heading.

Descend in the direction of Inishbofin and Horn Head, again noting the parallel lines of stones marking an old path. A pathless slope of bog and heather leads down to a track, which can be followed to the left to reach the R257 road on a moorland slope. Turn right to follow the road downhill, turning left to pass a school, then left again at a junction where a stone is marked 'Meenacladdy'. Follow this road down towards the sea, passing a few houses, then turn left up a clear bog road, rising from some gorse bushes over Cnoc an Duilisc. At a crossing of tracks, turn right and follow the track until it expires at the coast.

Turn left to walk along the coast, rising along the grassy edge of a bouldery clay cliff overlooking a rocky shore and storm beaches. Aim to link grassy strips with vague paths and tracks, keeping away from extensive turf cuttings further inland. There are little valleys to cross, and one of these is quite deep and carries a stream. The furthest headland is marked with a white concrete tower surmounted by a light. Continuing along the coast leads away from turf cuttings, across slopes of short grass, following a clear track to the next headland. When the track begins to climb uphill, look out for a small promontory fort off to the right. Cross a stile over a fence, then follow the track alongside a wall to reach a junction with a narrow

135

road. There is a memorial here recalling a drowning tragedy. Turn right to follow the road downhill, then the road climbs to the left and eventually reaches a junction with another road at Knockfola. Turn right to follow the road, rising on a bendy stretch to return to the Ocean Lodge B&B, or the car park beyond.

WALK 40

Tory Island

Although only a small island, Tory is immensely interesting and features a striking cliff-line. There are only two settlements, West Town and East Town. In ancient epic legends, Balor of the Baleful Eye, a formidable Formorian giant, is said to have inhabited a cliff-girt fortress at the eastern end of the island. The western end of the island has a lonely lighthouse. A round-the-island walk could be accomplished in a few hours, or you could spend a weekend or more exploring the place. Ferries run most often from Magheroarty, though in the winter months Tory can be cut off for days and weeks at a time.

The Route

Distance:	8 miles (13 kilometres).
Start:	West Town - 856465.
Map:	OS Discovery Sheet 1.
Terrain:	Roads, tracks, narrow paths or pathless cliff tops.
Parking:	Cars cannot be taken onto the island. Park near the pier at Magheroarty.
Transport:	Ferries to Tory Island run most often from Magheroarty, which is served by Lough Swilly Buses.

Leaving the Harbour at West Town, turn right to pass the Ostan Thoraidh, the church, school and an art gallery. When the houses peter out, follow the road across a rugged moorland to reach East Town. Keep left at a road junction; there is a B&B off to the right. Later, turn left along a track and cross a narrow neck of land where there is a rusty winch above a little pier. There is plenty of fine cliff scenery around the rugged promontory of Dún Balair. The jagged

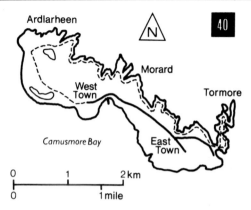

ridge leading to the final rocky tower of Tormore is particularly impressive. The highest point on the island is located on this promontory, crowned by a number of cairns. Views embrace Melmore Head and Horn Head, with hills rising inland including Muckish, the Aghlas, Errigal, Tievealehid and Slieve Snaght, ending with the hump of Bloody Foreland and other more distant features beyond.

Retrace steps back to the road and immediately start climbing up a heathery slope, pasing along the top of a fine cliff-line. A gentle desent leads around a rocky cove close to East Town. The cove is filled with strangely shaped sea stacks, arches and caves. There is an inlet passed later, and a deep blowhole just inland is known as St. Colmcille's Crater. The ground is bare and gritty, with rounded boulders of granite scattered around. After turning around another rocky cove a heathery slope leads to a summit bearing a cairn and a small metal structure. Looking towards the next headland, a series of deep clefts can be seen, so this is a good stance from which to plot the next few moves. Either stay faithful to the cliff-line or keep inland to pass all the inlets. Further along, a small slipway, cobbled track and steps are passed.

A solitary building is surrounded by the concrete anchors of a former transmitter mast. The view across the western end of Tory Island reveals a bouldery plateau and a lighthouse. Follow a grassy track down to a ruined building and turn right along a cobbly track to walk towards the lighthouse. There is no access to the compound, so turn left to follow a clear track away. The track passes a lagoon which is held by a storm beach, then fields are passed on the way back to West Town. Many of the island's facilities are passed on the walk back into the village, including the Caife an Chreagain and the 'Club'. Look out for a small ruined church to the right, and pass all the higgledy-piggledy buildings before reaching a shop, hostel, round tower, another shop and the pier.

Dún Balair

The cliffs which flank the rugged eastern end of Tory Island are truly awesome, and the promontory is approached easily only by crossing a couple of narrow necks of land. The rock scenery is impressive, and it's a wonder that the place isn't teeming with rock-climbers, especially the jagged ridge leading to Tormore. This amazing promontory was supposed to have been inhabited by Balor of the Baleful Eye; a Formorian giant whose very glance could slay a man dead. He was eventually killed by his own grandson Lugh of the Long Arms; a sort of Celtic solar deity.

Corncrakes

Tory Island is one of the last strongholds of the corncrake, whose 'crek-crek' call can be heard from the fields in the summer months. The corncrake always hides in tall grass, and so falls victim to modern cutting machinery in most parts of Ireland. On Tory, however, the farming is less mechanised and workers in the fields are less likely to cause injury to the birds.

WALK 41

Horn Head

Around a century ago you would have reached Horn Head either by taking a boat across the sea, or by walking across the sands at low tide. However, the former island is now joined to the mainland by a broad band of sand dunes and has easy access by road. There is a scenic loop road around the headland, allowing motorists to view the cliffs from a couple of places. Walkers, however, can leave the road and make sport all the way along the northern and eastern cliffs, which are quite dramatic, often overhanging or pierced by caves and arches.

The Route

Distance:	12 miles (20 kilometres).
Start:	Dunfanaghy - 017374.
Map:	OS Discovery Sheet 2.
Terrain:	Roads, followed by narrow cliff paths over heather, bog and grass slopes, ending with a forest track.
Parking:	Plenty of spaces around Dunfanaghy.
Transport:	Lough Swilly Buses serve Dunfanaghy.

This walk can be started in the village of Dunfanaghy, following the Horn Head road passing Holy Trinity Church of Ireland and a handful of B&Bs. After crossing Hornhead Bridge, the Forest Lodge B&B is passed and the road runs close to the shore. Keep to the right at a later junction. The road begins to rise from the shore, passing a number of houses and farms. The road continues over an open heather moorland, climbing to a stone shelter beside a viewpoint car park. There is a fine view back to Dunfanaghy, taking in the mountains of Muckish, the Aghlas and Errigal on the mainland. One last little house might be spotted just below, then the road descends and only a couple of ruined houses are in view, with long

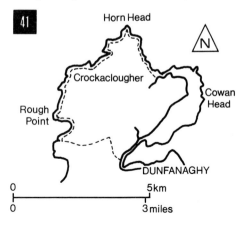

abandoned fields around them. The road rises to another stone shelter and viewpoint car park, where a line of fine cliffs are evident.

Leave the road to walk along the cliffs, following a series of vague paths through the heather, crossing some boggy patches. There is a fence along the cliffs, which needs to be crossed later in favour of a low ruined wall. When this feature expires, a sparse line of posts show the way ahead. The cliff line leads to a high headland, where there are three final prows; all steep sided and one with a strip of fencing. Looking down to the sea, wild goats might be spotted grazing. Retrace steps from the end of the headland, but keep to the right to follow another narrow, heathery cliff path. Views ahead reveal very blocky cliffs. An inlet forces a slight detour inland to cross a boggy little valley, where a gate in a fence is followed by another path.

Climb uphill from the valley, and the heathery slope gives way to another cliff path. A low wall can be followed onwards, passing a large, square-cut cleft in the cliff, then a fence can be followed onwards. The heather and grass become shorter as a headland is turned, and a wall has to be crossed. Do this at its seaward end with care, and note the fine arch cut into the base of the headland at the far side of a rocky cove. A path continues across a slope above a rocky shore, leading round Rough Point to Pollaguill Bay. Either cross the sandy beach, or walk along paths through the marram grass further inland. Cross a fence and continue around the next rugged slope, which also bears a vague path.

When a narrow, rocky inlet forces a move inland, continue climbing up a shallow valley, crossing a fence at the top. Keep to the right side of a boggy path to reach a forest, then follow a path straight through the forest to reach the corner of a track. Turn right to follow the track downhill. At first it is near the edge of the forest, but later it runs inside. A road is reached beside the Forest Lodge B&B, where a right turn leads back across Hornhead Bridge. Simply follow the road back to Dunfanaghy to bring the walk to a close.

WALK 42

Melmore Head

A recent blight of mobile homes and caravans has afflicted Melmore Head, but the walk around the headland can be structured so that they aren't too much of an intrusion on the scene. A high tide might restrict access to the beach walk on the eastern side of Melmore Head, but once ashore there are a number of vague paths which might be used. The northern and western sides of Melmore Head are quite rugged, and in clear weather there are some fine viewpoints embracing more of Donegal's headlands.

The Route

Distance:	8 miles (13 kilometres).
Start:	Rosses Strand - 117420.
Map:	OS Discovery Sheet 2.
Terrain:	Sandy and rocky shore walks require the tide to be out, while vague paths and rugged, pathless terrain occur elsewhere.
Parking:	A small car park is available at the Strand.
Transport:	There are no services nearer than Lough Swilly Buses to Milford and Creeslough.

There are no bus services to Melmore Head, north of Downings. Follow the road signposted for the Atlantic Drive, then take a road signposted for Melmore Head, followed by a left turn signposted for the Strand. There is a small car park at the end of this road. While there are plenty of mobile homes around, there is only a B&B and a youth hostel in the area. All other accommodation and facilities are back at Downings.

Leave the car park and follow the road back inland, turning left at a junction. The road is fenced at first, but after passing a stone cross, off to the right, it is possible to turn right across an area of unfenced grassland. When the sandy beach is reached, turn left to walk along the shore, but note that a very high tide might obstruct the way. If this is the case, you would need to follow the road towards the end of Melmore Head. The beach walk involves walking round a couple of small sandy bays, passing a small island, then

141

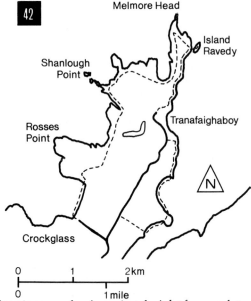

Melmore Head

Island Ravedy

Shanlough Point

Tranafaighaboy

Rosses Point

N

Crockglass

| 0 | 1 | 2km |
| 0 | | 1 mile |

continuing along a rocky shore. A rocky inlet forces a detour inland to the road, where a left turn leads over to another sandy beach at Tranafaighaboy.

Walk round the little bay and continue along a track through the final caravan site on the headland. Cross another small, sandy bay, then follow a path up from the far side, passing a gap in a fence, continuing across an open, grassy slope. The rather vague path passes a reedbed, where angular blocks of rock and some rusty winching gear are all that remain of a quarry. If the tide allows, then steps and bits of concrete indicate a path leading out onto Island Ravedy, which bears a white tower surmounted by a light. Steps need to be retraced afterwards.

Climb over the top of Melmore Head, walking on heather and low rock outcrops to reach a ruined stone tower. There are fine views of the Inishowen and Fanad peninsulas, as well as Horn Head and Tory Island in the other direction. Walk along the crest of the headland, passing a cairn and following vague paths and aiming towards the nearby caravan site. Go through a gate just before reaching the caravan site and climb straight uphill. Cross a fence and continue climbing, drifting to the right along narrow paths, keeping above the cliffs and rugged slopes overlooking a sandy beach. Descend gradually towards the shore and drift to the left to continue. The heathery, boggy ground can be quite flowery in summer, with many orchids. Cross two low walls and fences and pass a grassy peninsula on the lower slopes of Melmore Hill, walking over grassy ground above a rocky shore. After turning a rocky point a very rugged bay is seen, with several rocky points projecting seawards.

A narrow chasm forces a detour inland, then either cross a line of small hills, or keep inland from them to proceed. A fence and stone wall need to be crossed, and a couple of secluded sandy beaches can be seen below. Climb steeply uphill, exploiting a steep strip of grass between rocky outcrops. Either aim for a ruined lookout post on top of the hill, or cut across the slope and aim for a higher summit alongside. Grassy slopes and rocky outcrops give way to a rock and heather summit, where a fence is crossed to reach a cairn at 544ft (163m). There is a fine view of the peninsula, as well as Tory Island, Horn Head, the Donegal Highlands from Errigal to Muckish, and ranges of hills to Inishowen and Malin Head.

Turning right after crossing the fence gives the initial direction towards the sandy beach of Rosses Strand but there are also vague paths taking a more direct course. Choose any line which offers a clear run to the beach, avoiding rocky outcrops or patches of bracken. Walk to the far side of the beach, then come ashore, passing through a gap in a fence. A path leads straight back to the car park where the walk started.

WALK 43

Clonmany & Binnion

Binnion is a rugged little hill on the Inishowen peninsula, with its feet in the sea and its top offering a fine viewpoint. The walk can be based on either Clonmany or Ballyliffin; two villages crouching at the foot of the hill. Very high tides could make it difficult to get on and off the hill, as short beach walks are required. The ascent of Binnion is rather like a tough hill walk, which just happens to take place beside the sea. The route is structured to start with a road walk, but this can be omitted with the judicious use of a car, or by tying in with bus services.

The Route

Distance:	6 miles (10 kilometres).
Start:	Clonmany - 376463.
Map:	OS Discovery Sheet 3.
Terrain:	Roads at the start and finish, with steep, rugged, heather and rocky slopes between. The tide needs to be out around the foot of the hill.
Parking:	Plenty of spaces around Clonmany and Ballyliffin.
Transport:	Lough Swilly Buses serve Clonmany and Ballyliffin.

There are plenty of shops, pubs and cafes in Clonmany, as well as accommodation. A road junction beside the church is signposted for Ballyliffin. Follow this road uphill, passing a number of houses and B&Bs on the way to Ballyliffin. The road descends into the village, passing the Ballyliffin Hotel to reach the Strand Hotel. This

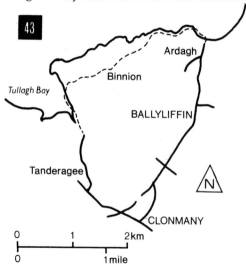

43

Ardagh

Binnion

Tullagh Bay

BALLYLIFFIN

Tanderagee

N

CLONMANY

0   1   2km

0   1 mile

first stretch of the walk has a bus service. Keep to the left of the Strand Hotel to follow a road down to Pollan Bay. The road is lined with houses and ends at a small car park where there is a children's play area. Beyond is the broad, sandy sweep of Pollan Bay, with Glashedy Island offshore.

A very high tide might make the next stretch of the walk impassable. Turn left and hug the rocky shore, walking on or beside a raised beach, noting small caves cut into the base of the low cliffs. Towards the end of the headland, it is possible to climb onto dry land and follow a fence uphill. There is a wide grassy strip between the fence and a series of spiky rock outcrops which project seawards. When the fence turns inland, beware of a deep, square-cut chasm which appears quite suddenly. Climb up a heathery slope, walking on low outcrops of rock, dodging scattered boulders, maybe following the course of a tumbled drystone wall. Proceed beyond the wall, over a shoulder, then climb more steeply to reach a cairned summit. This is not the highest point on Binnion, which is now revealed a little further away. Vague paths and tracks can be followed almost all the way to the higher summit, which bears a couple of cairns at 830ft (228m). Views stretch all around the Inishowen peninsula, taking in Malin Head and Dunaff Head, with Slieve Snaght, Bulbin, Raghtin More and the Urris Hills further inland. Other headlands and mountains can be seen to the west.

Descend westwards, taking care to keep away from rocky outcrops, seeking heathery slopes in preference to broken rock or bracken. There is a drystone wall near the top and bottom of the steep and rugged slope, then it is best to aim towards a low, rocky point at the mouth of the bay. The lower slopes are covered in spiky marram grass and a sandy track will be crossed before the shore is reached. Turn left to follow the track, which quickly descends to the sandy beach to avoid a couple of little cliff faces. Again, a very high tide could make this stretch impassable for a short while. Walk beside a tidal river, which is later accompanied by a path surfaced either with grass or gravel. Cross a footbridge, and continue inland along a narrow farm road. The road passes a row of caravans and a few houses, then reaches a junction with another road. Turn left, as signposted for Clonmany, and the village appears quite suddenly at the close of the walk.

Malin Head

Here's a walk with more than a hint of northern exposure, offering a loop around the most northerly part of the Irish mainland. This is a significant point, where the weather is constantly monitored and where a tidal gauge was used to determine Mean Sea Level for the most recent mapping surveys in Ireland. While only a short stretch of coastal path is available around the most rugged part of the peninsula, the road which loops around Malin Head offers a gentle walk with a satisfying amount of distance.

The Route

Distance:	8 miles (13 kilometres).
Start:	Crossroads Inn at Malin Head - 420576.
Map:	OS Discovery Sheet 3.
Terrain:	Mostly road walking, with an easy coastal path and track.
Parking:	Small spaces all around Malin Head.
Transport:	Lough Swilly Buses serve Malin Head.

Lough Swilly Buses pass the Crossroads Inn at Malin Head, which offers food, drink and accommodation. Follow the road past the nearby Country Cafe, walking straight onwards, avoiding two

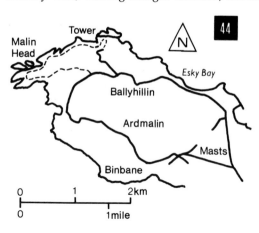

A little hut at Malin Head points to a visitor centre

roads off to the right. One road is signposted for the Seaview Tavern - 'Ireland's most northerly grocer, filling station and tavern'. The next road is signposted for Farren's Bar - 'Ireland's most northerly pub'. Yet another road to the right is signposted for a pier, but keep walking uphill to pass the Met Eireann Malin Head weather station. The road runs downhill and passes a stony beach at Esky Bay where the Curiosity Shop might be open.

An attractive huddle of cottages are passed at Ballyhillin, then a right turn is signposted for Banba's Crown - 'Ireland's Northerly Point'. Also to the right, if required, is The Cottage, offering teas, crafts, and a visitor centre. The road climbs uphill, reaching a parking place beside a prominent tower and some smaller ruined buildings. Views embrace a sea full of rocky stacks, stretching to the double-humped island of Inishtrahull. The hills and headlands of Inishowen rise inland from the Atlantic, while other hills and headlands can be seen further westwards.

Just below the tower is a headland marked with the word 'EIRE'. Follow a path off to the left, away from this headland, staying above the rocky shore and low cliffs. The path undulates and passes a short length of fencing at the head of a rocky chasm. The path passes other chasms as well as overlooking a row of rugged sea stacks. Cross a stile over a fence and walk along the headland as far as you like. A left turn leads onto a path and track which run by a curious building called Skildren Cottage. The track continues past a gravel pit and another house, eventually joining a road. Turn right to follow the road past a couple of farmhouses and a rocky beach, then climb uphill, passing a small viewpoint car park. The road runs across a rugged moorland, passing a scattered handful of houses. On the descent, note a road off to the right which is signposted for the Sandrock Hostel. Keep left, however, to follow the road straight back to the Crossroads Inn, passing the masts of a marine radio station.

Malin Head

Malin Head may be the most northerly point on the Irish mainland, but offshore is the double-humped island of Inishtrahull, which is even further north. The large ruined tower at Malin Head is a signal tower which was built to observe shipping around the coast. Both Lloyds and the British Admiralty had an interest in the place. The smaller structures date from the Second World War and are lookout posts. The word 'EIRE' can be seen marked out on the headland. This was to warn warplanes that they were flying over neutral Ireland. Aircraft which landed during that time were impounded and their pilots were interned.

WALK 45

Inishowen Head

Inishowen Head is a significant turning point, overlooking the mouth of Lough Foyle and the open Atlantic, taking in a spread of Scottish islands and whole ranges of Irish mountains. A short, circular walk is easily accomplished using quiet roads and moorland tracks. The route passes Portkill, where tradition maintains that St. Colmcille's last steps on Irish soil were taken before he founded an important monastery on the distant Scottish Isle of Iona.

The Route

Distance:	6 miles (10 kilometres).
Start:	Dunagree Point at Stroove - 682426.
Maps:	OS Discovery Sheet 3 & Discoverer Sheet 4.
Terrain:	Minor roads and easy moorland tracks.
Parking:	At White Bay at Stroove.
Transport:	Lough Swilly Buses serve Stroove.

Lough Swilly Buses run as far as Stroove and cars can be parked close to the lighthouse on Dunagree Point, beside the White Bay

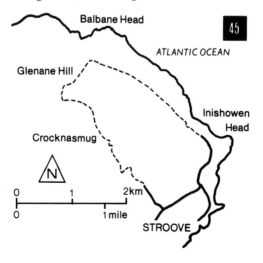

Take Away. Follow the road uphill and continue uphill along a narrower road at a junction. The road climbs past a farm and reaches a small parking space on Inishowen Head. There is an old lookout post on the headland, offering views of nearby cliffs and distant Scottish islands. Also in view are Rathlin Island, Benbane Head and the Antrim Mountains, with the seaside towns of Portrush, Portstewart and Castlerock followed by Binevenagh and the Sperrin Mountains.

The narrow road continues along the rugged cliffs, passing above Portkill, where there is a plaque telling about an ecclesiastical site below. The tarmac ends soon afterwards and a clear track continues, usually bounded by fences, flanked with bracken, heather or rough pasture. Cross a concrete bridge and continue climbing gently. When the crest of the track is reached, there is a view along the coast, and out to the remote island of Inishtrahull. The track descends and swings left, climbing again on an open moorland slope. A track to the right leads to a thatched cottage, so keep to the left. Another track to the right offers a continuation along the coast, but again keep left. The track climbs over the heather moorland and crosses another crest, with a view of Stroove below, and more distant features beyond.

Walk downhill on the track, zigzagging and keeping to the right to cross a bridge. Further downhill, turn left to follow another clear track, which runs downhill between fences. This track is later flanked by fuchsia and gorse, becoming surfaced in tarmac when it reaches a few houses. Turn left at the bottom to walk back into Stroove, returning to the White Bay Take Away and the lighthouse.

Portkill

St. Colmcille (generally known as Columba in Britain) is said to have taken his last steps on Irish soil at Portkill. He landed at the little bay, climbed onto the top of Cnoc an Leachta and took a last look at his native Donegal and Derry. Before leaving Portkill, he is said to have carved a cross on a stone slab with his finger. The cross-slab at Portkill, which may actually date from the 8th century, and a nearby holy well, are still visited on an annual pilgrimage.

WALK 46
Castlerock & Downhill

Castlerock is a small seaside resort close to Downhill, where the
National Trust have an interesting property. The ruins of a house
constructed by Frederick Hervey, the eccentric Earl Bishop of
Bristol and Derry, can be included in a short cliff walk. It could be
said that the sprawling Sperrin Mountains dip their toes into the sea
at Downhill and Castlerock. Walkers with a particular interest in
gardens and architecture will find that this walk abounds in interest.

The Route

Distance:	3 miles (5 kilometres).
Start:	Castlerock Railway Station - 774360.
Map:	OS Discoverer Sheet 4.
Terrain:	Easy paths, tracks and roads.
Parking:	Beside the sea at Castlerock.
Transport:	Northern Ireland Railways and Ulsterbus 134 serve Castlerock.

Leave Castlerock Railway Station and walk down towards the sea.
The road swings left in front of the Golf Hotel and there are parking
spaces alongside. A belt of dunes covered in marram grass hides a
broad, sandy beach from view. There is a chance to walk along a

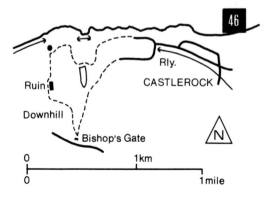

grassy strip above a low, rocky shore, but only as far as a small swimming pool. Follow another road further uphill, which swings left around a caravan park and is signposted as the Ulster Way. Turn right at a junction and follow a narrow road straight to a gatehouse beside the caravan park. There is a sign reading 'Black Glen Scenic Walks'.

Go through the gate and follow a clear path flanked by rhododendrons and other trees and shrubs. These close over the path to form a tunnel of vegetation, emerging in mixed woods with a view over a small dam and a peep through the glen mouth to the sea. The path should be followed straight onwards, keeping to the left to approach the Bishop's Gate and the main road. Don't go through the gate, but turn sharply right at a noticeboard and follow another path which becomes a broad, grassy track climbing to a gate and a grassy expanse. To the left is the Mausoleum, but the track runs to the imposing ruin of Downhill House. Ahead, the fine form of Mussenden Temple can be seen perched on the very edge of a cliff. Views from this point are wide ranging, stretching from the Giant's Causeway and Benbane Head to Inishowen in Co Donegal. The mouths of the Bann and the Foyle are also in view, while out to sea the Scottish islands of Islay and Jura can be seen in clear weather.

Turn right at Mussenden Temple, following a grassy path beside a cliff-top wall. The path runs downhill and turns inland, overlooking a railway tunnel beneath the caravan park. Cross a stile on the left before reaching a crenellated building. Steps lead downhill, and by walking past a small dam another path can be followed straight uphill. Turn left at the top, following a grassy path back towards the cliffs. The path veers to the right and leads to the caravan park. Walk along a track seaward of the caravans, passing a Coastguard building before joining a road near the small swimming pool. Simply follow the road straight back into Castlerock to return to the railway station. There are a few shops, pubs, restaurants, hotels and B&Bs.

Downhill

Frederick Hervey, the eccentric Earl Bishop of Bristol and Derry, built Downhill House from 1774 to 1791, extending and altering the structure for some years afterwards. His chief architect was Michael

Shanahan from Cork, assisted by Sir John Soane and Placido Columbani from Italy. At first the house was of dour appearance, being built of basalt, but it was later faced with sandstone. The building was burnt in 1851, but rebuilt and modified in 1870. Its final abandonment came after it was used by the RAF in the Second World War. The Bishop's Gate dates from 1784, and the Classical arch stands next to a Gothic gatehouse near the main road. Mussenden Temple was built between 1783 and 1785. It was based on the Temple of Vesta at Tivoli and was used as a library and summer house. It was named after the Bishop's cousin, Frideswide Mussenden.

WALK 47

Causeway Coast Path

The walk along the Causeway Coast Path between Carrick-a-Rede and Portballintrae must be the most interesting and varied coastal walk in Ireland. Cliff paths, beach walks, an amazing geology and wildlife are just some of the features along the way. Much of the coast is owned or managed by the National Trust, who are continually improving access while conserving its special heritage. Waymarking is in the form of hexagonal wooden posts, in the same style as the world-famous hexagonal stone columns of the Giant's Causeway.

The Route

Distance:	15 miles (24 kilometres).
Start:	Larrybane near Ballintoy - 052448.
Finish:	Portballintrae - 927420.
Map:	OS Discoverer Sheet 5.
Terrain:	A mixture of cliff paths and lower tracks, with some beach walks where high tides can be a problem.
Parking:	Larrybane, Ballintoy Harbour, White Park Bay, Dunseverick, Giant's Causeway and Portballintrae all have car parks.
Transport:	Ulsterbus 172 serves Ballintoy, the Giant's Causeway and Portballintrae, while Ulsterbus 252 is a summer service. Ulsterbus 138 and 177 run between the Giant's Causeway and Portballintrae.

There is a car park at Larrybane, east of Ballintoy, and bus services are also available. From April to September the celebrated Carrick-a-Rede Rope Bridge may be in service, which is worth experiencing. The path from the car park to Carrick-a-Rede is signposted and is easy to follow. Crossing the rope bridge calls for a good head for heights, as the structure is strung across a 60ft

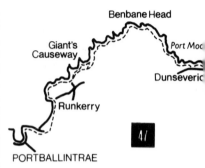

(20m) gulf some 80ft (25m) above the Atlantic. It links a large sea stack with the mainland for salmon fishermen, but most users are tourists. If it is open, then take a look, but steps have to be retraced afterwards to Larrybane. Omitting this spur would save 2 miles (3 kilometres). The Rope Bridge Tea Room and toilets are located at the car park, and paths allow an old quarry site to be explored with views of Sheep Island and Rathlin Island.

Continuing from Larrybane, a path runs along the cliff-tops, then cuts inland through fields to reach the prominent whitewashed Church of Ireland, which stands between Ballintoy village and harbour. Follow the road downhill from the church, round a series of corkscrew bends before landing at the harbour. Note the numerous rock stacks out to sea, and the caves cut deeply into the headland. There is a car park, toilets and old limekilns around the harbour, while Roarks Kitchen serves food and drink on the harbour wall.

Follow a track away from the harbour, passing a cottage, then continue along a grassy path. The sea is full of rock stacks, and some stacks are marooned on dry land. Look out for curious shapes, including stacks which have been pierced with holes large enough to walk through. A couple of stiles are crossed, and a spring can be seen issuing from beneath a large boulder. A short stretch of bouldery shore needs to be followed, where very high tides could be a problem, but normally the headland is easily passed.

White Park Bay features a couple of rashes of boulders, but is mostly a broad sweep of golden sand. Formerly there was a cliff

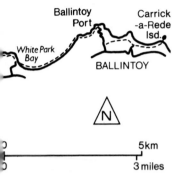

coast here, but it has been largely buried among sand dunes covered with marram grass. A few houses can be seen perched on top of the old cliff, while White Park Bay Youth Hostel sits at a lower level. Turning round the next chalk headland needs care, as the way is usually covered at high tide. Even when the tide is out, boulders and rock platforms can be slippery with seaweed. The tiny huddle of houses beyond is Portbraddan, with a miniature harbour and a little building claiming to be the smallest church in Ireland. It has a sign reading St. Gobban's, the patron saint of fishermen.

A path leaves Portbraddan, passing a few rock stacks, then proceeding through a hole in Gid Point. After passing a small waterfall, a series of stiles and steps lead the path along a rocky coast to reach another tiny harbour, car park and toilets. Follow the access road uphill, above the rocky shore, but look out for a flight of steps on the right allowing access back down to the next stretch of coastal path. The path leads around a grassy headland, then crosses a footbridge over a river. The rockier parts of Geeragh Point take the path towards Dunseverick Castle. The castle is on a naturally fortified headland and can be visited by a short diversion, heading down to a grassy gap before climbing up to the ruins. Leave by walking back down to the gap, then climb up a flight of steps. There is a car park beside the road nearby, and a noticeboard explains about the site.

The cliff path continues from Dunseverick, generally gaining height, but with some short, significant downhill stretches. Rugged headlands and bays can be studied, and there are fine views back towards Larrybane. This is a popular path and the National Trust have moved the fence back to allow more space for walkers. The path rises and falls, twists and turns, and eventually runs round Benbane Head to reach the dramatic viewpoint of Hamilton's Seat. The Inishowen peninsula can be seen, while the Scottish islands of

The Giant's Causeway seems to lead to a rocky peak

Islay and Jura may feature in clear weather. Traces of a lower path can be seen beneath the columnar cliffs, but this line has had to be closed following a rock fall. Keep to the cliff-top path, walking in and out, up and down, until a junction is reached with the Shepherd's Steps. Look out for fulmars and kittiwakes on the ledges, soaring ravens, merlins and sparrowhawks, as well as red-legged choughs.

A choice of route is available. Either keep to the top path and head straight for the Giant's Causeway Centre, or descend the Shepherd's Steps for more detailed explorations. The steps lead down a rugged slope to a junction with a lower path. Turning right leads to a dead end, but allows The Organ Pipes to be studied, and takes in the Port Reostan Viewpoint, close to where the Armada vessel 'Girona' was wrecked. Turning left leads past a rock known as the Giant's Boot to reach the celebrated Giant's Causeway and all its crazy columns. This is an immensely popular place, composed of tightly packed stone hexagons dipping towards the Atlantic. Looking inland, the cliff appears as a pyramidal peak, though this is an illusion as it is almost flat on top. A narrow road leads up to the Giant's Causeway Centre, where interpretative material and displays can be examined for a couple of hours. There is also a car park, restaurant, toilets and shop.

A path leaves the Giant's Causeway Centre along the cliffs towards Runkerry House. The path is gravel at first, becoming grassy later. It is forced inland to get round a deep chasm which the sea has cut into Runkerry Point. Runkerry House is the centre of a large building development, and the Causeway Coast Path keeps to its seaward side. There is a footbridge down near the beach which needs to be crossed, then a grassy path leads inland.

Turn right along the trackbed of an old tramway. This is a gravel track on an embankment, but there is a proposal to reopen the tramway and accommodate walkers alongside. Follow the tramway until a stout bridge over the Bush River can be seen, then head off to the right to follow a path through adjacent dunes instead. The course of the river leads to a long wooden footbridge near the mouth of the Bush River. Cross the bridge and bear right up a prominent path. After crossing a low headland of rock, a large car park and toilets are reached at Portballintrae. Walkers could arrange to be collected there, or could continue along the road to reach the bus stop. Follow the road past the Beach House Hotel, continuing above the harbour, passing a thatched cottage to reach a bus stop near the Bay View Hotel.

Ballintoy
The little village of Ballintoy is close to the start of the walk at Larrybane. There are a couple of shops and pubs, as well as accommodation, with a regular bus service. Easy access to both Larrybane and Carrick-a-Rede, or down to Ballintoy Harbour is available.

Dunseverick
This may have been an Iron Age stronghold, and was reputedly linked by a royal road to the Hill of Tara, once the political power-house of Ireland. Dunseverick may have been visited by St. Patrick in the 5th century, and the ancient kingdom of Dalriada may have been ruled from this point. All that remains of the early times are a few earthworks, and the headland was attacked by the Vikings in 871 and destroyed by them in 926. The ruins of a 16th century tower, looking like a rotten molar tooth on the headland, dates from a time of constant struggle between the Antrim families of MacDonnell, O'Neill, O'Cahan and MacQuillan.

Giant's Causeway
Nearly 40,000 hexagonal basalt columns make the Giant's Causeway an intriguing place to visit. National Trust wardens and minibuses run backwards and forwards between the causeway and the visitor centre, mixing scientific explanation with history, legends and downright lies! The visitor centre offers interesting displays and an audio-visual theatre, along with supporting literature and souvenirs. This is the place to check out the flora, fauna and geology of the Causeway Coast, as well as historical details such as the Armada ship 'Girona', which was wrecked nearby in 1588. There is a restaurant on site, as well as a car park and toilets.

Portballintrae
This little seaside resort can offer food, drink and accommodation at the end of the day, or a number of bus services for anyone wishing to leave. Just inland is the little town of Bushmills and its world-famous distillery, claiming to be the oldest legal whiskey distillery in the world.

WALK 48
Rathlin Island

Rathlin is the largest island off the northern coast; remarkably close to the Hebrides and Kintyre in Scotland. There are many connections with Scotland, ranging from Robert the Bruce to Caledonian MacBrayne ferries. The island is notable for its range of birds and flowers, while its geology is a curious mix of limestone and basalt. Rough roads and tracks run to three lighthouses and form the basis of a route exploring all three corners of the island. The only real settlement is Church Bay, which features an interesting interpretive centre.

The Route

Distance:	17 miles (28 kilometres).
Start:	Church Bay - 147500.
Map:	OS Discoverer Sheet 5.
Terrain:	Easy walking on roads and gravel tracks.
Parking:	On the mainland near the harbour at Ballycastle.
Transport:	Daily ferry services from Ballycastle. There is a minibus service on the island. Ulsterbus offers regular services to Ballycastle.

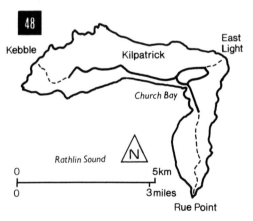

159

The route taken around Rathlin Island will depend on the time spent ashore, but the assumption is that the West, East and South Lighthouses will all be visited from Church Bay. This will involve retracing steps each time, but there is a minibus service which may be of use. The starting point for explorations is naturally the harbour at Church Bay. All the island's facilities are found here: small shops, post office, bar, restaurant, guest house, independent hostel, self-catering cottages, toilets and campsite. Of particular interest is the Boathouse Interpretive Centre, displaying the island's history, heritage, flora and fauna.

The walk starts by heading for St. Thomas' Church of Ireland, following a steep and narrow road uphill to St. Mary's Roman Catholic church. Turn left to follow another road uphill, noting a memorial to the right at the top of the road: 'An Gorta Mór 1845-1848. In memory of the 500 inhabitants of Rathlin Island who emigrated to America and England during the Great Famine.' The view at this point overlooks Church Bay and stretches wide to embrace Kintyre, Galloway, Fair Head, Slieveanorra, Knocklayd, Benbane Head and Inishowen.

The road undulates westwards and moves away from the sea, so that there are no coastal views. The road passes areas of moorland and rough grazing, as well as a couple of reedy pools. Beyond Cleggan the road is more patchy and as height is gained the sea again becomes visible. The last stretch of track is unfenced, rising from a small forest to cross a broad area of heather and gorse scrub, then crossing a cattle grid at the entrance to the Kebble National Nature Reserve. The reserve is mostly under short grass, with Kebble Lough at its centre and sheer cliffs falling to the sea on all sides. The West Light Seabird Viewpoint is usually open in the summer, offering the best views of the cliffs and their colonies of sea birds. Limited cliff-top walking can be enjoyed with care around Kebble, then afterwards steps need to be retraced to Church Bay.

On the return journey, when St. Mary's Roman Catholic church is reached, turn left at a road junction and follow the tarmac road towards the East Light. There is a junction with another road along the way, but keep straight onwards to pass through a gate, following a track onto a rugged heather moorland. The East Light can be seen ahead, and while it can be approached as far as its gates, there is no access beyond. Instead, there are tantalising glimpses to left and right of distant parts of Scotland. Turn around to follow the track back to the gate at the edge of the moor. Once the road is being followed, turn left at a junction, then turn right to follow the road back towards Church Bay. Left and right turns at the next couple of junctions lead down to McCuaig's Bar and Restaurant, where food and drink may be enjoyed before finishing the walk.

Leave the bar and follow the road to the post office and Boathouse Interpretive Centre. The road continues past a telephone and the Rathlin Guest House, then turns left to pass a toilet block. Keep to the track close to the rocky shore, noting a ruined building on the shore. Seals may be spotted along the shore, before the track turns inland near an old cornmill. Turn right at the next junction to follow a clear track towards the South Light on Rue Point. The track rises and falls gently, passing between Craigmacagan Lough and Kinkeel Lough. Next, Ally Lough and the larger Ushet Lough are to the right. The track continues to Ushet Point, where two ruined buildings stand off a grassy track. Continuing to Rue Point, the ground is more stony, and when bare rock is encountered a concrete path with a safety rail can be followed to the little lighthouse. Views take in Kintyre, Fair Head, Slieveanorra, Knocklayd, Benbane Head, Inishowen and Church Bay. Again, steps need to be retraced to Church Bay to bring the walk to a close.

Church Bay

All of Rathlin Island's facilities are clustered around Church Bay, and this is where food and drink and a limited amount of accommodation can be found. There are two churches; St. Thomas' Church of Ireland and St. Mary's Catholic Church. Both are left open and are worth visiting. The most imposing building was the Manor House built by the Gage family. Alongside is the old tithe barn, now known as the Richard Branson Activity Centre. Branson's involvement came after he was rescued when his first transatlantic ballooning venture ended prematurely off Rathlin Island. Seals can be spotted around Church Bay, including both common and grey. Oystercatchers and the occasional raft of eider can be spotted, as well as ringed plover and black guillemot. The rare thyme broomrape can be seen growing on drystone walls. In the summer months it is possible to enjoy round-the-island boat trips allowing fine views of otherwise unseen and inaccessible cliffs. Be sure to visit the Boathouse Interpretive Centre for a wealth of locally gathered information.

Kebble National Nature Reserve

The western end of Rathlin is an important nature reserve. Most people go there to view the populous colonies of seabirds, but there is also an interesting heath, grassland, lake and marsh. Dramatic cliff scenery includes a number of amazing stacks of rock and the best viewpoint is from the lighthouse, which may not always be open. Fulmars and kittiwakes are always present, while puffins regularly nest on the cliffs. Guillemots and razorbills are common, while inland it is worth looking for buzzards, peregrines, ravens, stonechats, skylarks, lapwings and wheatears. Tiny wrens can be seen in drystone walls on the way back to Church Bay. Orchids grace the lime-rich grasslands of Kebble, along with the rare limestone bugle, kidney vetch and sea campion. Irish hares might be spotted on the heath and grassland. Kebble Lough may be busy with gulls and ducks, as well as teal and heron.

East Light

Out of sight below the East Light, but visible from one of the round-the-island boat trips available in the summer, is Bruce's Cave. It is said that Robert the Bruce hid in this cave after his defeat at Perth. It is also claimed that he had his famous encounter with the spider, continually striving to weave its web. Inspired in this cave - 'If at first you don't succeed, try, try again' - he returned to Scotland and ultimate success at Bannockburn.

Rue Point

Two swift, surging tidal currents off Rue Point cause the formation of a whirlpool known as Slough na Morra - Swallow of the Sea. The Moyle is a notoriously turbulent stretch of water, with many violent currents and whirlpools which come and go according to the tides and weather. The last two buildings on the way to Rue Point are in ruins. One was used for smuggling and the other was used by coastguards. Seals are common on the low rocks.

WALK 49
Fair Head

When seen from Ballycastle, Fair Head assumes simple geometric lines. A level plateau gives way to a sheer cliff, then a bouldery slope angles neatly into the level sea. On closer inspection these simple lines are disrupted. The level plateau becomes a hilly area of rock, bog and heather. The sheer cliff is riven by gullies and chasms. The bouldery slope looks quite chaotic and the turbulent waters of the Moyle are upset by breaking waves and whirling eddies. Two short loops can be enjoyed on Fair Head and beside the shore at Murlough Bay.

The Route

Distance:	6 miles (10 kilometres).
Start:	High on the Murlough road - 191418.
Map:	OS Discoverer Sheet 5.
Terrain:	Rough and boggy paths, clear tracks and roads.
Parking:	Small car park high on the Murlough road, or down beside Murlough Bay.
Transport:	Ulsterbus 162A and 252 run no closer than Ballyvoy, offering only schoolday and summer services.

Murlough Bay is signposted from the main A2 road east of Ballycastle, but Ulsterbus services run no closer than Ballyvoy. The Murlough road climbs uphill on the slopes of Crockanore, then begins to descend. There is a small car park on the left and a notice explains about walks on Fair Head and around Murlough Bay. Basically, two loops are available; one around Fair Head and one around Murlough Bay. Start with the one around Fair Head.

Face the noticeboard and look uphill a short distance. Walk in that direction to pass through a gate and look out for yellow squares (not circles) painted on rocks. Little Lough Fadden will come into view on the undulating back of Fair Head and a couple of stiles are crossed. The route runs downhill towards an attractive huddle of whitewashed cottages at Coolnalough, beside Lough na Cranagh. Bear to the right and walk on the rugged hillside above the buildings.

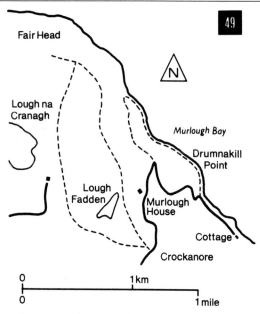

Do not go down to the farmyard. One of the islands in Lough na Cranagh is circular and buttressed with boulders. It is a crannóg, or ancient defended lake dwelling.

Look carefully across the hillside for yellow circles painted on rocks. These indicate a path climbing towards the cliffs of Fair Head. The path crosses patches of bog, heather and bare basalt rock. The cliffs appear quite suddenly, dropping sheer to a bouldery scree so take care. There is a fine viewpoint from a prominent boulder perched on the very edge of the cliff. Across the turbulent waters of the Moyle, Rathlin Island and the Mull of Kintyre are often in view. You could turn left or right to explore along the cliff tops, but you need to turn right to return to the car park.

A fairly clear path marked by yellow circles leads back towards the car park. On the way, make little detours to see more sheer cliffs, detached pinnacles of rock, awesome gullies and narrow chasms. There is only one breach in the cliff, where the steep and rocky Grey Man's Path descends beneath a wedged bar of rock. Stay high on the cliffs, which become less steep and more vegetated with ivy and trees. After passing Lough Fadden and crossing stiles, the path ends back at the car park.

Follow the narrow road downhill for the Murlough Bay loop. The hairpin road is on a grassy and wooded limestone slope, passing Murlough House, tucked neatly into a hollow. There is a small car park on the next hairpin bend, where a clear track to the left should be followed. This becomes a fine grassy line descending across a rugged slope. It appears to lead onto the chunky, bouldery scree at the base of Fair Head, but watch carefully to spot a less clear grassy track to the right. This track leads to a couple of ruined colliery buildings and expires. Pick a way along a rough, bouldery, grassy slope, which seems set to become very rough at Drumnakill Point. However, a fine path is joined at that point and it leads to a narrow road.

Turn left along the road to explore Murlough Bay. The road quickly becomes a track and passes through a gate. A limekiln, a small bothy and a house are reached towards the end. It is necessary to retrace steps, then follow the road steeply uphill in a series of tight hairpin bends. Murlough House is passed again on the way back to the car park at the top of the road. If a pause for breath is needed, there are many places on the ascent offering fine views around the bay.

Fair Head and Murlough Bay

The National Trust manage Fair Head and Murlough Bay and although the area is small the range scenery and wildlife habitats are impressive. Geologically, Fair Head is a thick bed of basalt resting on limestone, with some coal mesures which were worked for a short time. The rugged headland features several ancient structures, including a crannóg, or fortified lake dwelling, a hill fort, chambered grave and cairns. It is claimed that the headland takes its name from a beautiful Rathlin woman, victim of jealous suitors, who was eventually flung into the sea from the island and washed ashore at this point on the mainland.

WALK 50

Whitehead & Black Head

Whitehead is a little town on the northern shore of Belfast Lough, while Black Head is a rugged cliff crowned by a lighthouse. Regular bus and rail services reach Whitehead, from where an easy path runs towards and around Black Head. Flights of concrete steps run up the cliff face to reach a lighthouse, then more steps lead back downhill. This remarkable and popular path offers a short, safe and spectacular outing in good weather.

The Route

Distance:	3 miles (5 kilometres).
Start:	Whitehead Railway Station - 475918.
Map:	OS Discoverer Sheet 15.
Terrain:	Black Head is rocky, but the path and steps used are concrete.
Parking:	At the end of the promenade.
Transport:	Northern Ireland Railways and Ulsterbus 163.

If reaching Whitehead by rail or bus services, walk down to the promenade and turn left. Towards the end there is a car park for anyone arriving with a vehicle. The path running onwards is entirely surfaced in concrete and is perfectly clear to follow without the need for detailed route directions.

The beach below the path is cobbly, with occasional large boulders, while the slopes rising inland are vegetated with scrub and shrubs. There are benches and shelters along the way, then after the path passes a couple of houses the rugged cliffs of Black Head begin to dominate the scene. The path remains easy and proves to be a great feat of engineering. In places the rock has been cut back to accommodate the concrete walkway and there are overhangs and caves, footbridges across chasms, stout barriers and safety fencing.

There are parts of the path which may be engulfed by waves during stormy weather. After turning all the way around Black Head, climb up flights of steps which zigzag back and forth across the rocky slope. Take them steadily to avoid reaching the top a

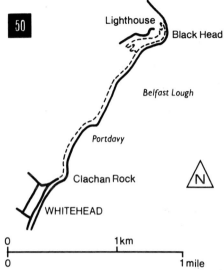

lobstery hue! There is a lighthouse on top of Black Head and the path passes in front of it, between tall stone walls. Views take in the length of Belfast Lough, stretching over the North Channel to the Galloway Hills of Scotland and possibly to the distant Isle of Man.

Continue following the path, which runs parallel to the lighthouse access road for a short way. The path then descends through patches of scrub on a steep slope, with more flights of steps. After some zigzagging, the cliff path joins the lower path which was used earlier. Turn right to pass the two houses noticed earlier in the walk and retrace steps to the promenade at Whitehead. There are options to use paths rising up the scrubby slope to return to Whitehead.

Whitehead

This small seaside town sits on a low gap between White Head and Black Head, offering food, drink and a choice of accommodation. The railway line pierces White Head and close to the station is the headquarters of the Railway Preservation Society of Ireland. Steam engines and static displays can be studied every Sunday in July, while the Portrush Flyer sometimes runs steam-hauled excursions.

Black Head Path

A commemorative stone at the start of the path reads: 'Berkeley Deane Wise 1853-1909. Railway Engineer and Architect. Designer for Whitehead Promenade, Black Head Path, Gobbins Path.' The path was reconstructed in 1993 and repaired after extensive rockfall damage in 1998.

WALK 51

North Down Coast Path

The North Down Coast Path runs along the southern shore of Belfast Lough between Holywood and Groomsport. It stays low, but runs very close to the sea using a variety of paths, tracks and roads, passing through the Crawfordsburn Country Park and the seaside resort of Bangor. The stretch between Holywood and Crawfordsburn is part of the Ulster Way, but the coastal path extends as far as Groomsport. There are plenty of bus and train services a short distance inland, making this one of the most approachable and adaptable coastal walks in Ireland.

The Route

Distance:	12¹/₂ miles (20 kilometres).
Start:	Holywood - 398793.
Finish:	Groomsport - 537836.
Map:	OS Discover Sheet 15.
Terrain:	Low level paths, tracks and roads.
Parking:	Car parks at Holywood, Crawfordsburn, Helen's Bay, Bangor and Groomsport.
Transport:	Ulsterbus 1 & 2 serve Holywood and Bangor. Ulsterbus 3 serves Bangor and Groomsport. Northern Ireland Railways serve all stations between Holywood and Bangor.

Walkers starting in the centre of Holywood can admire a tall maypole; said to be the tallest permanent maypole in the world. Follow Shore Road down to a busy dual carriageway road, cross over, then go under a railway bridge to reach the shore of Belfast Lough. Turn right as indicated by an Ulster Way signpost to follow a concrete promenade path equipped with benches. Views across Belfast Lough take in the Belfast Hills. The promenade runs parallel to the

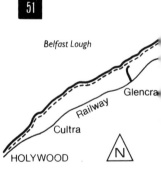

railway, then branches away across a stretch of grassy parkland. Ferries and flights in and out of Belfast can be observed. Pass a small pier and slipway at Cultra Avenue and walk past the Royal Northern Ireland Yacht Club on Seafront Road. The road continues as a gravel track, while the Ulster Folk and Transport Museum rises for some distance inland, spanning both the railway and main road.

The coast path runs along the top of a wall for a short distance, then passes the end of Glen Road. A concrete path beside garden walls leads to another narrow shore road. The path continues beside a tall fence bounding a golf course, then turns round a low, rocky, wooded point. Look out for Halftide Rock, which could have seals hauled out on it, or cormorants using it while drying their wings. The path continues beside a tall wall at Rockport, where the path has been built up above the level of the beach. After passing a wooded point the path rises gently through an area of scrub and bracken, running seawards of the Seahill Sewage Treatment Works.

Follow the path through an arched gateway, then a flight of concrete steps lead uphill over a wooded cliff, before more steps lead down to the shore again. A gravel path beside a rocky shore leads into the Crawfordsburn Country Park. This is one of the busiest countryside sites in Ireland. Walk past a boathouse and continue around a small bay, passing the end of a road which leads to the village of Helen's Bay. Blue waymark arrows show the way through the country park, but they are hardly necessary as the way ahead is so obvious. After passing through a turnstile the path runs

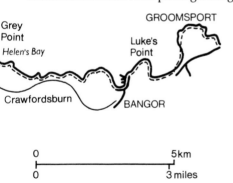

along a low cliff-line on the wooded Grey Point. A sign indicates the Grey Point Fort, which can be visited if desired. The path wanders through a wood before reaching another road running into the village of Helen's Bay.

A broad promenade path leads around Helen's Bay, proving

popular with strollers and well equipped with benches. Views across Belfast Lough now feature the peninsula of Islandmagee and part of the Rhinns of Galloway in Scotland. A broad gravel track continues over a low, wooded point to reach the next part of the Crawfordsburn Country Park. There is access inland to a fine visitor centre and restaurant. The Ulster Way moves inland to Crawfordsburn, but the course of the North Down Coast Path continues towards Bangor and Groomsport.

Cross a footbridge over the burn, then follow the coastal path round a rocky, wooded point to pass a large, derelict house. The path continues across a sandy beach, where a very high tide could be a problem, but normally the way will be clear. After turning the next wooded point, a concrete and tarmac path around Swineley Point passes a golf course. Beyond Smelt Mill Bay, the path passes the end of Brompton Road and follows a tarmac path below a prominent tower. After turning a low cliff-line, the route approaches the seaside resort of Bangor. The towers of St. Comgall's Church of Ireland and the First Presbyterian Church rise over the town. There are plenty of facilities and amenities around the harbour and marina, with many places offering food and drink. There are plenty of accommodation options in town. At the far side of the harbour is the old Tower House which is where the tourist information office is located. Only small fragments of the old town survive, and to most people Bangor has the air of a Victorian seaside resort.

Follow a promenade path out of Bangor, with views across the mouth of the lough to the Mull of Kintyre and Isle of Arran in Scotland. After turning round the grassy Luke's Point and passing Ballyholme Yacht Club, a tarmac path continues around Ballyholme Bay to reach a car park and children's play area. The tide needs to be out as the route continues across the sands close to a sea wall, but only for a short while, coming ashore again at the end of the wall. Ballymacormick Point is a stretch of coastal heath and scrub managed by the National Trust. The path is grassy or gravel, surrounded by gorse and brambles in places. As Groomsport is approached, a narrow road can be followed, or a path can be used to reach the harbour. There are places offering food and drink, while buses can be used to reach Bangor, where onward bus and rail connections can be made.

Holywood

The maypole in the centre of Holywood has been replaced many times since at least 1700, when a ship ran aground on May Eve and its mast was used as a maypole. However, a plan of the town dating from 1625 shows something like a maypole on the same site. There are plenty of places offering food and drink, as well as a range of accommodation.

Cultra

The Ulster Folk and Transport Museum is a vast open-air museum in the grounds of Cultra Manor. Many fine buildings have been rescued from ruin all around the countryside and rebuilt stone by stone on this site. A visit is highly recommended, but it takes a whole day to explore the place properly. There is no immediate access to the folk park from the shore.

Grey Point Fort

The fort dates from 1904 and was built to defend Belfast Lough against invaders, serving through two world wars. It is open to visitors at certain times and its huge guns have been preserved. Carrickfergus Castle, on the opposite side of Belfast Lough, played a similar role in earlier centuries. Paul Jones and the fledgeling American Navy took Carrickfergus by surprise in 1778. A skirmish with HMS Drake is regarded as America's first naval victory!

Crawfordsburn Country Park

A short walk inland leads to the Crawfordsburn Visitor Centre, where a variety of displays tell about the flora and fauna of the country park. This is one of the busiest countryside sites in Ireland. Other short walks include the Meadow Walk and the Glen Walk with fine waterfalls. There is a restaurant, car park and toilets on site.

Groomsport

Groomsport is notable as the point where Schomberg landed in 1689 with 10,000 Williamite troops at his disposal, heralding a series of battles culminating in the Battle of the Boyne in 1690. The little harbour is now a quiet place offering food and drink at the end of the day's walk.

WALK 52

Strangford Lough

Strangford Lough is an enormous marine lough fed and emptied twice daily by the tides. All the water for the lough flows back and forth between Strangford and Portaferry. Amazingly, there is a regular ferry service across the turbulent strait. The National Trust manages Strangford Lough as an important wildlife scheme, and near Strangford they own the old Castle Ward estate. A coastal walk is available around Strangford and Castle Ward, ending with a woodland walk and a road walk back into town.

The Route

Distance:	7¹/2 miles (12 kilometres).
Start:	Strangford - 588497.
Map:	OS Discoverer Sheet 21.
Terrain:	Easy paths, tracks and roads by shore and woodland.
Parking:	In the centre of Strangford and at Castleward.Transport: Ulsterbus 16E serves Strangford.

Leaving the centre of Strangford, a little town which repays exploration, follow Ulster Way signposts from The Square along Castle Street. Strangford Castle is to the right, a 16th century tower house, but keep to the left to continue to the gateway for Old Court. Turn left at the gateway to discover the appropriately named Squeeze Cut. Steps take this narrow path uphill between tall walls, then it runs downhill between high brambly banks to reach a track beside Strangford Lough. Turn left along the track, noting the curious round bathing tower beside the water.

Follow the track into woods, then turn right along a track signposted for the Strangford Bay Path. Turn left to follow the path along a rugged shore, which might be underwater during very high tides. The path can be a bit rough underfoot, but it is mostly level, passing woods and fields before turning round a pine-clad headland. A track is joined, which is followed to the right to reach the main A2 road at Down Lodge. Turn right, follow the road, using the footway provided, to reach an entrance for Castleward Caravan Site.

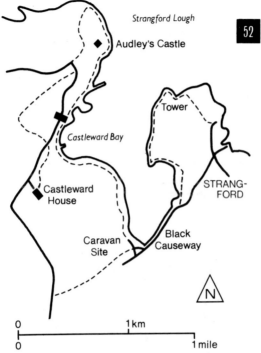

52

Walk along a narrow road through an imposing gateway, then keep to the right to follow a woodland track onwards. The woods are dense in places, delightfully mixed, with an understorey of rhododendron, bramble and ivy. Views may be restricted, but for birdwatchers there is access to the Eagleson Hide on the shore, overlooking the Castleward Bay Refuge Area. Further along, there is a junction of tracks and a series of signposts list various destinations and attractions on the estate. Follow the track to a tarmac road and turn right, descending past the Strangford Lough Wildlife Centre. Some wonderful buildings are reached, including Old Castle Ward and The Cornmill.

Walk through an arched gateway after exploring, to follow a track signposted as the Ulster Way. This runs through woods to

Castleward is one of the features near Strangford

reach the Strangford Sailing Club. A wooded and grassy path continues around a point crowned by Audley's Castle. Follow a woodland path round the point to emerge facing the other side of the castle. Turn right along a track to reach a gate and a junction, then turn left down towards three semi-detached buildings called Green Row. Turn right to walk away from the buildings, not by road, but by following a track from a black gateway. The track runs past the narrow Temple Water, turning left around the head of the pool. A grassy path leads through an avenue of young trees, then a sign points the way to the House and Stableyard. The path goes under an archway and is known as the Laurel Walk, leading up through another arch to Castleward House.

If the house is to be explored, then access to it is through the Stableyard. If the building is closed, or if a visit is not to be made, then follow the narrow tarmac road away to the right, turning left at the next junction. As the road climbs, there are a couple of glimpses left to Castleward House. The road is called Ballyculter Avenue and it runs towards a gatehouse called Ballyculter Lodge. Don't pass the lodge, as this leads back onto the main road. Instead, turn left beforehand down a woodland track, which descends to the Castleward Caravan Site. Turn right to reach the gate used earlier in the walk, then turn left to follow the main A2 road straight back to Strangford. If time can be spared, then include a ferry ride across to Portaferry and have a look around the Exploris Centre.

Strangford Lough

The Vikings named this place Strang Fjord, or the Violent Fjord, after the turbulence of the straits. St. Patrick was swept through in its currents and stepped ashore to start his great mission near Raholp, rather than from Antrim as originally intended! The foreshore of the lough is managed as a wildlife scheme and the rest as a marine nature reserve. The lough is an important site for wildfowl and waders, especially brent geese. Seals can be observed around the narrows, especially from the Cloghy Rocks. Otters and eels are common and there are around fifty small islands dotted around the lough. Plenty of background information can be obtained from the Strangford Wildlife Centre on the Castle Ward estate.

Castle Ward

Now a property of the National Trust, the Ward family originally developed this estate and left it with some bizarre features. A huddle of old stone buildings can be inspected around the shores of Castleward Bay, including Old Castle Ward and the Cornmill, as well as Audley's Castle. Castleward House is set further inland, with one front being classical in design and the other being Gothic. Bernard and Anne Ward simply couldn't agree on one style, and their architect had to accommodate them both. The house has an enclosed stableyard and the surrounding gardens are well worth exploring.

Portaferry
Although not on the walk, Portaferry is easily approached by taking the ferry across the narrows of Strangford Lough, despite the powerful tidal race! Portaferry and Strangford complement each other nicely, facing each other across the turbulent waters. Exploris is the name of a superb aquarium which offers the chance to see some of the creatures which inhabit Strangford Lough and the Irish Sea. One of the most interesting items is a 'touch tank' where it is possible to feel and handle a number of living exhibits.

WALK 53

Killough & Ballyhornan

The Lecale coast features a couple of interesting coastal paths around Killough, Ardglass and Ballyhornan. Road walking is currently necessary to link them, but in the future it is likely that short link paths will be developed. The low, rocky shore gives way to rough grassland before cultivated fields stretch further inland, and in the summer an amazing variety of flowers can be enjoyed. The walking is easy and as there are places along the way offering food and drink, the route lends itself to a leisurely appreciation.

The Route

Distance:	12 miles (19 kilometres).
Start:	Killough - 538361.
Finish:	Ballyhornan - 592420.
Map:	OS Discoverer Sheet 21.
Terrain:	Low level paths and roads. Some paths can be muddy.
Parking:	Car parks at Killough, Ardglass and Ballyhornan. Transport: Ulsterbus 16A serves Killough, Ardglass and Ballyhornan. Ulsterbus 16B also serves Ballyhornan.

Killough has a central car park and bus service, though it is also possible to be dropped off at St. John's Point and thereby omit the

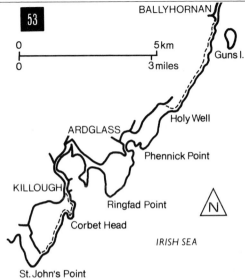

initial road walk. Leave Killough by following the road called Fisherman's Row, signposted for St. John's Point and the Ulster Way. Towards the end of this road, turn right up Point Road, then follow the road as it rises and falls gently through a landscape of farms, fields and hedgerows. Note the prominent dome of Slieve Donard in the distance. Turn left at a road junction to reach St. John's Point, passing close to the ancient ruins of St. John's Church just before reaching the coast. To the right is a black and yellow banded lighthouse, but the route turns left as indicated by a public footpath signpost.

Cross the stile to start following the footpath over muddy ground. The path is sparse in places, but you can look ahead to spot stiles or waymark posts to keep on course. The route is always on the rough strip of land between the rocky shore and cultivated fields. Some parts are muddy and other parts feature gorse bushes, but the course of the path is generally easy throughout. The path runs close to a farm, then later crosses a cobbly storm beach before turning around a grassy headland dominated by a stout whitewashed building. After passing the building, follow a narrow road straight back into Killough along Fisherman's Row.

The main A2 road out of Killough is signposted for Ardglass. This is Castle Street; a fine, tree-lined avenue passing pubs, shops and colourful cottages. Pass The Square and continue along the coast road, keeping to the right at a junction on the edge of town. Note an old railway engine house to the left, and the course of an old trackbed which still features bridge buttresses where it crosses a tidal inlet. The road twists and turns to cross the same inlet, passing the reedy Strand Lough and climbing uphill past the Coney Island Caravan Park. After passing signs for Coney Island (which may one day have its own coastal path) climb to the right up Green Road and descend to the harbourside at Ardglass.

Ulster Way signposts point to the left to lead walkers around the harbour, passing a fine little castle and other crenellated buildings. Pubs, shops, restaurants, B&Bs and toilets are all passed, and there is a car park beside the Phennick Cove Marina. The A2 continues as Strangford Road, signposted to the right on the way out of town. Also to the right on the edge of town is a short field path climbing to the ruins of Ardtole Church, dedicated to St. Nicholas, offering a fine view of the surrounding countryside.

Turn right along Sheepland Road, which is signposted for St. Patrick's Well, then turn left at the next junction to continue. Further along, to the right, another signpost reveals a hedged, grassy track leading down to the sea where a left turn leads straight to St. Patrick's Well. Around St. Patrick's Day, the way is bright with gorse, primrose, daisies and marsh marigold. Two small wells and a large crucifix stand in a concrete enclosure.

Follow the shore onwards, crossing a stile. Rocks are covered in thrift and lichen, then a series of ruins, including an old windmill tower, are noticed around Sheepland. Later, a white house on a headland of gorse and heather is passed, then a gradual climb on grassy slopes leads to the top of Benboy Hill. Views stretch along the low, rocky coast, inland to the Mountains of Mourne and Slieve Croob, with Guns Island just offshore and the Isle of Man also visible in clear weather. The path passes between high and low fields, then drops downhill to pass another low field. Continuing closer to the sea, it passes a few houses on a track, then joins a narrow road. Follow the road into the village of Ballyhornan, climbing uphill towards the end to reach the Cable Bar, or follow a concrete path up to a car park.

Killough
For a short time Killough was known as Port St. Anne and had a busy harbour, windmill, limekiln and brickworks. The harbour was used by the Ward family of Castle Ward, to avoid having to pay harbour dues in Strangford. There are three interesting little churches, Roman Catholic, Church of Ireland and Methodist, as well as Victorian cottages and almshouses.

Ardglass
Although still an important port, Ardglass was once the busiest little port in Ulster. Jordan's Castle stands near the harbour and there are seven tower houses and fortified storehouses around the village. After suffering severe damage in the 1641 Rebellion some of the trade switched to neighbouring Killough.

Ballyhornan
There are buses away from Ballyhornan if a return has to be made to Killough, Ardglass or Downpatrick. The Cable Bar is available for a drink. Short strolls nearby could include a visit to Guns Island while the tide is out, or a short walk around Killard Point, which has a wide variety of flowering plants and orchids. Back along the road, Sheepland Farm Visitor Centre provides a view of farm life and includes a reconstructed rath farmyard.

WALK 54

Dundrum & Murlough

Much of the coast around Clough, Dundrum and Newcastle is owned by the National Trust. Dundrum Bay is open sea, but Dundrum Inner Bay is sheltered by the extensive Murlough Dunes. Walking along the coast is accomplished using a disused railway trackbed between Clough and Dundrum, switching to dune paths around Murlough, ending with a beach walk to Newcastle. The towering form of Slieve Donard, where the Mountains of Mourne 'sweep down to the sea', dominates landward views.

The Route

Distance:	8 miles (13 kilometres).
Start:	Clough - 410400.
Finish:	Newcastle Bus Station - 378316.
Maps:	OS Discoverer Sheets 21 & 29.
Terrain:	Low level tracks, roads and paths. The beach walk may be impassable at high water.
Parking:	There are small parking spaces around Clough, more spaces around Dundrum and ample parking at Newcastle.Transport: Ulsterbus 17, 20 and 240 serve Clough, Dundrum and Newcastle.

The walk is linear and there are plenty of bus services between Clough and Newcastle. If a car is used, it may be more convenient to park it at Newcastle, catch the bus to Clough, then walk back to Newcastle. Clough is a small village with an inn and a couple of shops, as well as an interesting motte and bailey offering a panoramic view of the surrounding countryside. While Clough is not actually on the coast, there is easy access by road to Dundrum Inner Bay. Simply follow Blackstaff Road, which is signposted for Ardglass, then turn right along Ardilea Road after passing the entrance to a timber mill. At a lower bend in the road, steps on the left lead up to an old railway trackbed alongside Dundrum Inner Bay.

Turn right to cross an old stone bridge and follow the trackbed along an embankment. The old line is owned by the National Trust and is called the Dundrum Coastal Path. It is part of the Ulster Way. The trackbed is mostly grassy and is flanked by gorse and brambles, but becomes more wooded further along. Dundrum Inner Bay broadens and a bridge is crossed where the tide floods a small lagoon backed by a large farm. Look out for herons and a variety of waders in this area. Ahead are the domed profiles of Slieve Donard and Slieve Commedagh in the Mountains of Mourne. Later, the trackbed is again more wooded with less of a view across the bay.

The Dundrum Coastal Path quickly comes to an end when it runs into the busy A2 coastal road near Dundrum, after passing a small reed bed and proceeding along an embankment of gorse and

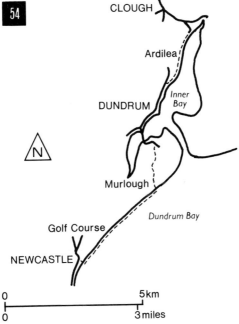

54

CLOUGH

Ardilea

Inner Bay

DUNDRUM

N

Murlough

Dundrum Bay

Golf Course

NEWCASTLE

```
0                    5km
|--------------------|
0                    3miles
```

brambles. Follow the main road into the village, passing two green spaces to the left. First is the gaelic football ground, followed by the Dundrum Boat Park Recreation Area. A number of shops and pubs offer food and drink, occurring just in time for a lunch break.

When leaving Dundrum, look out for a grassy path opposite St. Donard's Church, which is marked with a small National Trust sign. The path is short and well wooded, and is again based on the old railway trackbed beside Dundrum Inner Bay. When a minor road is reached, turn left to follow it out onto Keel Point and cross the lovely stone arches of Downshire Bridge. The road passes the Gate Lodge and continues along The Avenue, which is lined by trees and has a path running parallel. When the road runs into more open country, look out for a prominent gate on the right.

Go through the gate and follow a grassy track alongside a series of fenced-off fields. The fields are to the right, near Murlough Farm, while to the left are hummocky, well-vegetated dunes forming the Murlough National Nature Reserve. The track is known as the Back Track and later there are a series of small, yellow marker posts which need to be followed away from the fence. These markers reveal a winding dune path which has a grassy and sandy surface. After taking a roller-coaster ride over the dunes, turn right alongside another fence and go through a gate. A sandy path leads to a marker post perched on the last dune before the beach. Turn right to walk along the beach. A very high tide might make this stretch impassable, but only for a short time. There is no danger of being cut off along the way, as other prominent white marker posts indicate paths leading back inland.

The beach at low water is quite firm sand, becoming more shingly on the way to Newcastle. Timber groins have helped to stabilise the beach, while the dune belt has been protected either by more timber or by bouldery banks. On the final approach to Newcastle, Slieve Donard really begins to dominate the forward prospect, with the seaside resort huddled at its foot. After passing a more substantial concrete sea wall, come ashore beside the Slieve Donard Hotel. This impressive red brick building features attractive gables and a fine, central tower. Follow Station Road straight inland to reach the bus station. The old railway station is now the Spar shop. There are abundant accommodation options around Newcastle, as well as plenty of pubs, restaurants, cafes and shops. The tourist information centre and Mourne Countryside Centre are at the southern end of town, closer to the foot of Slieve Donard.

Clough
Clough Castle is an Anglo-Norman motte and bailey with the remains of a small tower, dating from the early 13th century. The short climb to the tower reveals a fine view embracing the coast, the Mountains of Mourne, Slieve Croob and the rolling Downshire countryside. The village of Clough has few facilities, offering the Clough Inn and Frenchies Restaurant, as well as a couple of shops.

Murlough National Nature Reserve
The National Trust own the Murlough Dunes and have managed them as Ireland's first nature reserve since 1967. Stone Age

settlements have been discovered beneath the sands, and some of the dunes are so well vegetated that they have become covered in woody scrub. A variety of habitat types include hazel and buckthorn scrub, a flowery heath, areas of marram grass, sheltered mudflats and a sand and shingle foreshore. Dundrum Inner Bay is an important wintering area for brent geese, waders and ducks, while the open sea supports other ducks and divers, as well as seals. The dunes support a varied flora, ranging from marram, heather and bracken to rare bee orchid, viper's bugloss, and more common wild pansies and bird's-foot trefoil. Animals include rabbits, foxes and badgers, with insects such as moths and butterflies, including the rare marsh fritillary. Birds on the dunes range from skylark and meadow pipit to reed bunting and stonechat, with willow warblers, finches and thrushes also abundant. Shelduck nest in old rabbit burrows, while ringed plover use the beach.

OTHER IRISH BOOKS PUBLISHED BY CICERONE PRESS

THE MOUNTAINS OF IRELAND *Paddy Dillon*
A necessary sequel to the Nuttalls' Mountains of England & Wales. All the Irish peaks given in detail.
ISBN 1 85284 110 9   PVC cover   228pp   £9.99

THE IRISH COAST TO COAST WALK *Paddy Dillon*
A wonderful walk from Dublin and the Wicklows to Valencia Island on the Kerry coast, linking various trails.
ISBN 1 85284 211 3   168pp   £7.99

CICERONE PRESS have a large selection of guidebooks which cover most of Britain, many of the popular walking areas of Europe and worldwide. Below are listed a selection of the books in Wales, the Lake District, Northern England and Scotland

ACROSS NORTHERN ENGLAND
THE MAJOR LONG DISTANCE TRAILS

WALKING THE CLEVELAND WAY & THE MISSING LINK *Malcolm Boyes*
The circular tour of the North York Moors, including some of our finest coastline.
ISBN 1 85284 014 5   144pp   £6.99

THE DALES WAY *Terry Marsh* A practical handbook to a very popular walk. With Accommodation Guide. *ISBN 1 85284 102 8   136pp   £6.99*

THE ALTERNATIVE PENNINE WAY *Denis Brook & Phil Hinchliffe*
The APW goes from Ashbourne in Derbyshire to Jedburgh in the Borders, 431 km. Milder than the official PW and much pleasanter to walk. *ISBN 1 85284 095 1   272pp   £8.99*

THE ISLE OF MAN COASTAL PATH *Aileen Evans* The coastline is of exceptional beauty. The Raad ny Foillan path encircles the island; the Herring Way and Millennium Way are also described. *ISBN 1 85284 277 6   152pp   £7.99*

THE PENNINE WAY *Martin Collins* By popular demand, Cicerone has produced a guide to the Pennine Way. Thoroughly researched by one of our most expert authors, this gives everything you need to know about Britain's first LD Trail. *ISBN 1 85284 262 8   144pp   £6.99*

LAUGHS ALONG THE PENNINE WAY *Pete Bogg* Anyone who has struggled through the bogs of the PW will identify with the humour of this cartoon book. Ideal gift.   *ISBN 0 902363 97 2   104pp   £3.99*

THE ALTERNATIVE COAST TO COAST *Denis Brook & Phil Hinchliffe* From Walney Island on the edge of the Lake District to Holy Island in Northumberland, across some of Britain's finest hill country. *ISBN 1 85284 202 4   272pp   £9.99*

A NORTHERN COAST TO COAST WALK *Terry Marsh* The most popular LD walk in Britain, from St Bee's to Robin Hood's Bay. Includes accommodation guide. *ISBN 1 85284 126 5   280pp   £7.99*

MOUNTAINS OF ENGLAND & WALES
- for the collector of summits

THE RELATIVE HILLS OF BRITAIN *Alan Dawson*
You've heard of the Munros - here are the Marilyns - all the mountains and hills in Britain which rise more than 500ft above their surroundings. *ISBN 1 85284 068 4 A5 size 256pp £8.99*

THE MOUNTAINS OF ENGLAND & WALES *John & Anne Nuttall*
Vol 1: WALES   *ISBN 1 85284 036 6 256pp PVC cover £10.99*
Vol 2: ENGLAND *ISBN 1 85284 037 4 320pp PVC cover £11.99*
Over 400 mountains in England and Wales attain 2,000 feet and it is an ambition of many walkers to climb them all. These are the definitive lists, with detailed route descriptions and delightful pen drawings.

LAKE DISTRICT & MORECAMBE BAY - Guide Books

CONISTON COPPER MINES: A Field Guide *Eric G. Holland* For mine explorers and the visitor or hill walker. *ISBN 0 902363 36 0 120pp £4.99*

THE CUMBRIA WAY AND ALLERDALE RAMBLE *Jim Watson.* A guide to two popular Lake District long distance walks done in Jim's inimitable style. *ISBN 1 85284 242 3 £6.99*

THE EDEN WAY *Charlie Emett* A walk through a romantic part of Cumbria. Can be broken into sections by using the popular Settle-Carlisle railway.   *ISBN 1 85284 040 4 192pp £5.99*

THE LAKE DISTRICT ANGLER'S GUIDE *Laurence Tetley* Following his successful guide for anglers in Yorkshire the author gives all details for fishing in the Lake District. Clubs, shops, permits etc. - an indispensible guide. *ISBN 1 85284 283 0 248pp £10.99*

SHORT WALKS IN LAKELAND *Aileen & Brian Evans*
Book 1: SOUTH LAKELAND *ISBN 1 85284 144 3 328pp £10.99*
Book 2: NORTH LAKELAND *ISBN 1 85284 232 6 328pp £10.99*
Around 60 walks in each book, on the lower fells and dales, described, mapped and illustrated in detail. Highly acclaimed. OWG/COLA Best Guidebook 1997

SCRAMBLES IN THE LAKE DISTRICT *R.B. Evans*
ISBN 0 902363 39 5   192pp PVC cover £9.99
MORE SCRAMBLES IN THE LAKE DISTRICT *R.B.Evans*
ISBN 1 85284 042 0 200 pp PVC cover £9.99 Exciting rock scrambles in gills or up crags, to thrill the mountaineer.

THE TARNS OF LAKELAND VOL I: WEST *John & Anne Nuttall* *ISBN 1 85284 171 0 240pp £9.99*

THE TARNS OF LAKELAND VOL 2: EAST *John & Anne Nuttall* *ISBN 1 85284 210 5 200pp £9.99* Lakeland Book of the Year prize winner 1996. Walks to delectable tarns. Illustrated by John's superb drawings.

WALKING ROUND THE LAKES *John & Anne Nuttall* The ideal walk encompassing all the major summits, yet with high and low level alternatives. *ISBN 1 85284 099 4 240pp £6.99*

WALKS IN THE SILVERDALE/ARNSIDE AONB *R.B. Evans* A well illustrated guide to short walks in this delightful area on the fringe of the Lake District.Fully revised. *ISBN 0 902363 78 6 168pp £6.99*

WINTER CLIMBS IN THE LAKE DISTRICT
Bob Bennett,Bill Birkett , Brian Davison Packed with the latest routes which confirm the area as a major winter climbing venue when conditions allow.
ISBN 1 85284 246 6 200pp £14.99

NORTH-WEST ENGLAND outside the Lake District

FAMILY WALKS IN THE FOREST OF BOWLAND *Jack Keighley.* 30 walks written and illustrated in the author's unique manner. *ISBN 1 85284 251 2 72pp Wiro bound £5.99*

WALKING IN THE FOREST OF BOWLAND *Gladys Sellers* Despite the limited access in this AONB moorland area, there are some beautiful walks.
ISBN 1 85284 154 0 168pp £6.99

LANCASTER CANAL WALKS *Mary Welsh* A guide to circular walks based on the canal, beautifully illustrated by Christine Isherwood. *ISBN 1 85284 138 9 120pp A5 £5.99*

A WALKER'S GUIDE TO THE LANCASTER CANAL *R. Swain* Preston to Kendal, including the branch to Glasson Dock, together with the fascinating history of the canal. *ISBN 1 85284 055 2 124pp £5.99*

WALKS FROM THE LEEDS-LIVERPOOL CANAL *Mary Welsh* 34 circular walks based on the canal. Illustrated by Christine Isherwood's superb drawings.
ISBN 1 85284 212 1 144pp £7.99

THE RIBBLE WAY *Gladys Sellers* From sea to source close to a junction with the Pennine Way. *ISBN 1 85284 107 9 112pp £5.99*

WALKS IN RIBBLE COUNTRY *Jack Keighley* 30 family walks, with maps and diagrams all beautifully drawn. Pocket size, spiral binding. *ISBN 1 85284 284 9 72pp £5.99*

WALKING IN LANCASHIRE *Mary Welsh* 39 walks described on a seasonal basis. Illustrated superbly by David Macaulay and Linda Waters. *ISBN 1 85284 191 5 160pp A5 size £6.99*

WALKS ON THE WEST PENNINE MOORS A Companion Guide to the Recreation Area *Gladys Sellers* A guide to the popular Lancashire Pennines.
ISBN 0 902363·92 1 192pp £5.99

WALKS IN LANCASHIRE WITCH COUNTRY *Jack Keighley* 30 family walks with maps and diagrams all beautifully drawn. Pocket size, spiral binding.
ISBN 1 85284 093 5 72pp Card cover £5.99

THE PENNINES & NORTH-EAST ENGLAND

CANOEISTS' GUIDE TO THE NORTH-EAST *Nick Doll* Covers the rivers of S.E. Scotland, Northumberland, Durham and Yorkshire - plus the coastline. *ISBN 1 85284 066 8 272pp £7.99*

HADRIAN'S WALL Vol 1: The Wall Walk *Mark Richards* In 22 stages Mark conducts you along the wall, accompanied by his skilful maps and sketches.
ISBN 1 85284 128 1 224pp £7.99

HADRIAN'S WALL Vol 2: Wall Country Walks *Mark Richards* 29 circular walks which incorporate the Wall, illustrated with Mark's sketches. *ISBN 1 85284 209 1 200pp £7.99*

WALKS FROM THE LEEDS-LIVERPOOL CANAL *Mary Welsh* 34 circular walks based on the canal. Illustrated by Christine Isherwood's superb drawings. *ISBN 1 85284 212 1 144pp £7.99*

NORTH YORKS MOORS Walks in the National Park *Martin Collins* A definitive guide. *ISBN 0 902363 87 5 240pp £6.99*

THE REIVER'S WAY *James Roberts* 150 miles around Northumberland. *ISBN 1 85284 130 3 112pp £6.99*

THE TEESDALE WAY *Martin Collins* A walk which follows the Tees from its source to the sea. 100 miles, 8 stages. Also includes 10 circular walks. *ISBN 1 85284 198 2 112pp £7.99*

WALKING IN COUNTY DURHAM *Paddy Dillon* Day walks, cycleways and LD trails in a landscape rich in heritage. *ISBN 1 85284 216 4 £7.99*

WALKING IN THE NORTH PENNINES *Paddy Dillon* The exhilarating moors between the Yorkshire Dales and Hadrian's Wall. *ISBN 1 85284 084 6 200pp £6.99*

WALKING IN NORTHUMBERLAND *Alan Hall* Mountain, moorland and sandy coast. Some of the most secluded and finest walking in England. *ISBN 1 85284 265 2 200pp £9.99*

WALKING IN THE SOUTH PENNINES *Gladys Sellers* The area between the Dales and the Peak District. Rich in industrial heritage. *ISBN 1 85284 041 2 400pp £10.99*

WALKS IN THE NORTH YORK MOORS Bk 1
Jack Keighley ISBN 1 85284 134 6 72pp
WALKS IN THE NORTH YORK MOORS Bk 2
Jack Keighley ISBN 1 85284 197 4 72pp
WALKS IN THE YORKSHIRE DALES - Book 1
Jack Keighley ISBN 1 85284 034 X 72pp
WALKS IN THE YORKSHIRE DALES - Book 2
Jack Keighley ISBN 1 85284 065 X 72pp
WALKS IN THE YORKSHIRE DALES - Book 3
Jack Keighley ISBN 1 85284 085 4 72pp
30 family walks in each book, with maps and diagrams all beautifully drawn. Pocket size, spiral binding. *£5.99 each*

WATERFALL WALKS - TEESDALE & THE HIGH PENNINES
Mary Welsh Remote waterfalls, beautifully illustrated by Linda Waters. *ISBN 1 85284 158 3 A5 £5.99*

THE YORKSHIRE DALES A Walker's Guide to the National Park *Gladys Sellers* A comprehensive survey of the best walking in the Yorkshire Dales. *ISBN 1 85284 097 8 328pp £10.99*

THE YORKSHIRE DALES ANGLER'S GUIDE *Laurence Tetley* A com-prehensive guide on where to fish, how and where to obtain tickets or licences what baits to use etc. *ISBN 1 85284 260 1 232pp £9.99*

WALES Long Distance Trails

THE LLEYN PENINSULA COASTAL PATH *John Cantrell.*
Starting at Caernarfon the coastal path goes round the peninsula to Porthmadog following the old Bardsey Pilgrims' route. Described for walkers and cyclists, with additional day walks. *ISBN 1 85284 252 0 168pp £8.99*

WALKING OFFA'S DYKE PATH *David Hunter* Along the Welsh Marches, 170 miles from Chepstow to Prestatyn. *ISBN 1 85284 160 5 224pp £8.99*

THE PEMBROKESHIRE COASTAL PATH *Dennis R. Kelsall* One of Britain's most beautiful paths. 181 miles in 15 stages, includes circular walks, and accommodation guide. *ISBN 1 85284 186 9 200pp £9.99*

SARN HELEN *Arthur Rylance & John Cantrell* The length of Wales in the footsteps of the Roman legions. *ISBN 1 85284 101 X 248pp £8.99*

WALKING DOWN THE WYE *David Hunter* 112 mile walk from Rhayader to Chepstow. *ISBN 1 85284 105 2 192pp £6.99*

A WELSH COAST TO COAST WALK- Snowdonia to Gower *John Gillham* An ideal route for backpackers, away from waymarked trails. *ISBN 1 85284 218 0 152pp £7.99*

WALES

ASCENT OF SNOWDON *E.G. Rowland* The six paths to the summit. Revised. *ISBN 0 902363 13 1 32pp £1.99*

ANGLESEY COAST WALKS *Cecil Davies* Short, easy walks around the varied and historically interesting coast of the island. *ISBN 1 85284 266 0 104pp £6.99*

THE BRECON BEACONS *Davies and Whittaker* 33 routes described in detail with a commentary on everything seen along the way. Instructive and practical. *ISBN 1 85284 182 6 200pp £9.99*

CLWYD ROCK *Gary Dickinson.* Rock climbs in the Welsh Border. *ISBN 1 85284 094 3 232pp PVC cover £14.99*

HILL WALKING IN SNOWDONIA *Steve Ashton* Routes which appeal to today's hill walker, illustrated with many of Steve's exceptional photographs. *ISBN 1 85284 008 0 120pp £7.99*

HILLWALKING IN WALES Vol 1: Arans - Dovey Hills *ISBN 1 85284 081 1 256pp*
HILLWALKING IN WALES Vol 2: Ffestiniog - Tarrens *ISBN 1 85284 082 X 272pp*
Peter Hermon. A comprehensive alphabetical guide to all the mountains and lakes of Wales. *£7.99 each*

THE MOUNTAINS OF ENGLAND & WALES Vol.1: WALES *John and Anne Nuttall ISBN 1 85284 036 6 256pp PVC cover £10.99*

THE RIDGES OF SNOWDONIA *Steve Ashton* Not just another guide! A mixture of descriptions, essays and photographs which convey the spirit of the route. *ISBN 0 902363 58 1 248pp £8.99*

SCRAMBLES IN SNOWDONIA *Steve Ashton* The classic rock ridges and other adventurous routes up challenging rocky faces. Second edition. *ISBN 1 85284 088 9 168pp PVC cover £9.99*

SNOWDONIA WHITE WATER, SEA AND SURF - Canoe Guide *Terry Storry* The white water rivers, the coastal canoeing and surf beaches of North Wales.
ISBN 0 902363 77 8 160pp £5.99

SPIRIT PATHS OF WALES *Laurence Main* Draws on Welsh lore and legend, literature and history around ley lines - spirit paths. 20 unique routes. *ISBN 1 85284 289 X*

WELSH WINTER CLIMBS *Malcolm Campbell & Andy Newton* The snow and ice climbs of North Wales. Superb diagrams and colour photos. *ISBN 1 85284 001 3 256pp PVC cover £14.99*

SCOTLAND

WALKING IN THE ISLE OF ARRAN *Paddy Dillon* 41 day walks in this 'Scotland in Miniature'. *ISBN 1 85284 269 5 200pp £10.99*

THE BORDER COUNTRY - A Walker's Guide *Alan Hall* 53 walks in the Border Hills and Southern Uplands. *ISBN 1 85284 116 8 232pp £7.99*

BORDER PUBS & INNS - A WALKER'S GUIDE *Alan Hall* 53 pubs and inns with complete details of food, beers, access for children etc. and a suitable short walk based on each. *ISBN 1 85284 172 9 168pp £6.99*

THE CENTRAL HIGHLANDS 6 LONG DISTANCE WALKS *P.D.Koch-Osborne* Classic backpacking routes. *ISBN 1 85284 267 9 200pp £9.99*

CAIRNGORMS Winter Climbs *Allen Fyffe* Covers the best winter climbs in the Cairngorms, Lochnagar and Creag Meaghaidh. *ISBN 0 902363 99 9 120pp PVC cover £7.99*

WALKING THE GALLOWAY HILLS *Paddy Dillon* The wilderness hills of Galloway in southern Scotland. *ISBN 1 85284 168 0 168pp £7.99*

WALKING IN THE HEBRIDES *Roger Redfern* General descriptions and suggestions for walking routes in these varied, delectable Western Isles. *ISBN 1 85284 263 6 184pp £9.99*

WALKS IN THE LAMMERMUIRS, with Moorfoots, Broughton Heights and Culter Hills *Alan Hall* The lonely, stimulating hills between the River Tweed and Edinburgh. *ISBN 1 85284 214 8 216pp £9.99*

WALKING IN THE LOWTHER HILLS also Carsphairn Hills, the hills of Solway Coast, Tinto, and Cauldcleugh Head *Ronald Turnbull* Completes the Cicerone coverage of walking in Southern Scotland's hills *ISBN 1 85284 275 X 184pp £8.99*

NORTH TO THE CAPE *Denis Brooke & Phil Hinchliffe* A new walk from Fort William to the North Cape described in the authors' inimitable way with masses of maps and drawings. This will become a collector's item. *ISBN 1 85284 285 7 208pp £10.99*

THE ISLAND OF RHUM - A Guide for Walkers, Climbers and Visitors *Hamish M.Brown* The complete companion for any visitor to the island, owned by the Nature Conservancy. *ISBN 1 85284 002 1 100pp £6.99*

THE ISLE OF SKYE - A Walker's Guide *Terry Marsh* Walks in all parts of the island, from simple outings to rugged days in isolated situations, yet without scrambling. *ISBN 1 85284 220 2 216pp £9.99*

THE SCOTTISH GLENS *P.D.Koch-Osborne £6.99 each*
Book 1: CAIRNGORM GLENS *ISBN 1 85284 086 2 128pp*

Book 2: THE ATHOLL GLENS *ISBN 1 85284 121 4 144pp*
Book 3: THE GLENS OF RANNOCH *ISBN 1 85284 170 2 144pp*
Book 4: THE GLENS OF TROSSACH *ISBN 1 85284 199 0 144pp*
Book 5: THE GLENS OF ARGYLL *ISBN 1 85284 226 1 144pp*
Book 6: THE GREAT GLEN *ISBN 1 85284 236 9 144pp*
Book 7: THE ANGUS GLENS *ISBN 1 85284 248 2 144pp*
Book 8: KNOYDART TO MORVERN *ISBN 1 85284 282 2 144pp*
Book 9: THE GLENS OF ROSS-SHIRE *ISBN 1 85284 296 2 144pp*
The popular series of guides for walkers and mountainbikers.

SCOTTISH RAILWAY WALKS *H.M.Ellison* All the old lines are walked and nostalgically remembered. *ISBN 1 85284 007 2 192pp £6.99*

SCRAMBLES IN LOCHABER *Noel Williams* Some of the best scrambling in Britain around Glencoe and Ben Nevis and much of the Western Highlands too. *ISBN 1 85284 234 2 192pp £9.99*

SCRAMBLES IN SKYE *J.W.Parker* The Cuillins is a paradise for scrambling. *ISBN 0 902363 38 7 144pp PVC cover £7.99*

SKI TOURING IN SCOTLAND *Angela Oakley* 51 great ski-tours in all parts of the Highlands. *ISBN 1 85284 054 4 208pp £6.99*

TORRIDON - A Walker's Guide *Peter Barton* A comprehensive guide to this wild but beautiful area. *ISBN 1 85284 022 6 168pp £7.99*

WALKS from the WEST HIGHLAND RAILWAY *Chris & John Harvey* 40 walks, linear between stations or circular, based on a day's return travel from Glasgow. *ISBN 1 85284 169 9 £6.99*

THE WEST HIGHLAND WAY *Terry Marsh* A practical guide to this very popular walk. *ISBN 1 85284 235 0 112pp £6.99*

WINTER CLIMBS BEN NEVIS & GLENCOE *Alan Kimber* Britain's finest winter climbing area. *ISBN 1 85284 179 6 232pp PVC cover £14.99*

CICERONE PRESS

A FULL CATALOGUE IS AVAILABLE FROM
Cicerone Press, 2 Police Square, Milnthorpe, Cumbria,
LA7 7PY. Tel: 01539 562069
E-mail: info@cicerone.demon.co.uk
Web Site: www.cicerone.demon.co.uk